101

Successful Ways To Turn Weekends Into Wealth

Also by the Author

How to Earn Over $50,000 a Year at Home
How to Make Your First Quarter Million in Real Estate in Five Years
How to Make $100,000 a Year Selling Residential Real Estate

101

Successful Ways
To Turn Weekends
Into Wealth

Dan Ramsey

Parker Publishing Company, Inc.
West Nyack, New York

Library of Congress Cataloging in Publication Data

Ramsey, Dan
   101 successful ways to turn weekends into wealth.

   Includes index.
   1. Success—Case studies.   I. Title.
HF5386.R1545   650.1'2   80-14629
ISBN 0-13-634808-4

To my chosen kin—The Richards, et al.

What This Book Can Do For You

This book will show you how to make $200, $500, $1,000, $2,000 and more in *extra cash* every month by turning your weekends—or any spare time—into wealth and security.

On the way, you'll meet over one hundred successful Weekend Wealth Builders who have one thing in common—they wish to repay our commerce system for its generosity. And they're doing it by sharing their hard-earned secrets of success with *you*. Many of them are revealing trade secrets to others for the first time. Others are offering you little-known techniques that have made them thousands of dollars.

KEYS TO THE GOLDEN CIRCLE OF WEALTH

These successful Weekend Wealth Builders will show you:

* How to start your own profitable Weekend Wealth Venture with *little or no capital.*
* How to *automatically* choose the most successful—and profitable—idea from dozens of opportunities.
* How to turn everyday skills into quick profits *this weekend.*
* How to tell *thousands* of potential customers about your product or service *free of charge.*
* How to *stop wasting time* and move right up to the Golden Circle of Wealth.
* How to profit from more than *one hundred* unique Weekend Wealth Ventures.

Plus, there are dozens of other time-saving and wealth-building techniques that can quickly move you up to the top of the ladder of success with just a few hours of your spare time.

HUNDREDS SHOW YOU HOW

Every opportunity—every successful wealth venture—is detailed for you by the people who made them work. You'll watch:

* Phyllis S. turn the Power of Leverage into a 300 percent profit
* Steve S. strike a gold mine with his Wealth Building Blocks
* Orville C. turn a simple idea into an extra $600 a month
* Dennis G. save $4,000 by using my system for testing Venture Profitability
* Don L. develop a completely risk-free Weekend Wealth Venture with one simple technique
* Nell H. multiply her profits by 1700 percent by adding a link to the Market Chain
* Ed J. discover Buyer Buttons that give him an easy $200 profit every weekend

IT'S YOUR TURN

Need extra cash? Looking for an easy retirement income that doesn't require much of your time? Want to start saving *now* for your dream home? You can begin adding thousands of extra dollars to your bank account soon by investing a day off, a weekend or a few evenings a week into one of these *proven* Weekend Wealth Ventures.

Here's your opportunity to discover more than one hundred unique and *highly successful* ways to turn your spare time into quick, easy money.

Dan Ramsey

Contents

Chapter 3
How Weekend Wealth Builders
Create Dynamic Profit Ventures Fast - 47

Chapter 4
Ten New Methods For Activating
Your Weekend Wealth Venture
With No-Risk Capital - 65

Chapter 5
Activating Your Weekend Wealth Venture
With High Profit Power Tactics - 83

Chapter 6
How Smart Weekend Wealth Builders
<u>Guarantee</u> Their Fortunes - 101

Chapter 7
Using The Power Of Dynamic Motivation To Multiply Your Profits - 117

Chapter 8
Weekend Wealth Building Techniques That Quickly Overcome And Neutralize Competition - 133

Twelve Ways You Can Turn Your Weekends Into Wealth **Now**

Let's be honest. You picked up this book for one—or both—of two reasons:

* You're looking for more money! You're tired of having too much *month* left at the end of the *money*. You want some extra income and you want it quick!
* You're looking for a challenge! You're weary of letting the boss make a profit on you and want to try a part-time enterprise that could buy your freedom from the time clock.

Congratulations! You've taken your first step on your road to financial freedom and success. This book offers you not only the practical and proven step-by-step system for turning weekends into wealth, it also introduces you to more than one hundred successful Weekend Wealth Builders who will tell you exactly how they did it. In the coming pages you may meet someone in your own town—in your own neighborhood—who has turned his spare hours and every-day skills into extra cash and has the satisfaction of being his own part-time boss. They will share their secrets on how you can join them as a Weekend Wealth Builder.

GENERATING SUCCESS WITH YOUR WEEKEND WEALTH PLAN

The dynamic Weekend Wealth Plan that you're about to discover can help you reach nearly any goal you set for yourself. With it you can find:

* *Money.* You can add $100, $200, $500 a week or more to your income with little or no starting capital.
* *Security.* You can begin pyramiding your savings account to $5,000, $10,000 or more for security against any emergency and peace of mind for the future.
* *Challenge.* You can expand your horizons and put more enjoyment into every day of your life with the challenge of your new enterprise.
* *Success.* You can feel the exhilaration of success as you work toward your own goal.

The Weekend Wealth Plan will show you exactly how to make it happen for you: How to choose your own goals; How to set up your weekend enterprise; How to turn your skills into quick cash; How to find time to start and expand your venture profitably. You'll be guided each step of the way by ambitious people like yourself who have successfully turned their weekends into wealth.

EARNING BIG MONEY WITH YOUR WEEKEND WEALTH VENTURE

A Weekend Wealth Venture is an enterprise that can turn your spare hours—one or two days or a few evenings a

week—into quick and easy profits. All you need for a successful Weekend Wealth Venture is:

* Spare time
* Everyday skills
* A profitable idea

The purpose of this book is to show you exactly how to
develop each of these three commodities and blend them
into a successful Weekend Wealth Venture that can bring
you the money and personal satisfaction you desire.

The main reason for a Weekend Wealth Venture is, of
course, wealth. You're looking for a way to trade a few extra
hours for some easy cash. You want to catch up on some old
bills, or buy a newer car, or stuff some money away for
retirement. For whatever reason, you want to find out how to
turn your spare time into profit.

It's easy. All you have to do is apply Ramsey's Rule of
Profits:

Money finds the person who fills a need.

In other words, you can earn extra cash by finding a
basic need or desire in people—one that they're willing to
pay someone to fill—and fill it. That's how your grocer, your
gas station owner, your television repairman and your own
boss earn their profits. And that's how you will earn yours.
Let's meet our first Weekend Wealth Builder and see
Ramsey's Rule of Profits in action.

How Harold W. Earns Big Money With His Weekend Wealth Venture

Harold W. of Conway, Arkansas, discovered his
Weekend Wealth Venture while talking across the fence to a
neighbor. His neighbor, Fred M., was complaining about
having to cut the grass every week. "Heck, I'd pay someone
five dollars a week if they'd cut it for me—and it wouldn't
take more than 20 minutes."

Harold saw a need.

He went to the other people in his neighborhood and
asked each of them if they would be willing to pay five
dollars a week to have their lawn mowed regularly. With one

exception they all said they would. That made six lawn cutting jobs in his neighborhood alone. He estimated that the six would take about two hours a weekend and earn him $30—$15 an hour!

After a couple of weekends of earning some easy cash, Harold began canvassing nearby streets with his lawnmower and gas can. On a typical Saturday Harold was earning $75 to $100. Then Harold got even smarter. He signed up regular accounts, rented extra lawnmowers and hired responsible teenagers to do the actual cutting at three dollars an hour. It was good work for them and it provided easy profits for Harold.

Today Harold earns $200 to $250 every weekend with his lawnmower service—even when he's out fishing. Best of all, he started with no capital—just his own lawnmower and a need. Harold is a smart Weekend Wealth Builder.

BREEDING SECURITY WITH YOUR WEEKEND WEALTH VENTURE

It's a great feeling to know that you have enough cash in the bank to cover the many emergencies that can arise. You can take care of needed auto repairs before they become too expensive. You can afford adequate insurance to protect yourself from medical or financial bankruptcy. You can take advantage of golden opportunities.

Security is also knowing that you have an alternative. It's facing a factory or industry layoff as an opportunity rather than a tragedy. It's not having to depend on your boss for every dollar you make. It's knowing that you have many marketable skills that will give you a good living in any economic situation. Security breeds self-confidence.

Your Weekend Wealth Venture can give you the security you desire while still offering you the regular pay check of your full-time job. Let's see how one Weekend Wealth Builder earned both kinds of security in just a few hours each week.

How Vernon T. Traded Fear For Security With His Weekend Wealth Venture

Vernon T. has worked in the same paper mill in Eureka, California, for the last 22 years. During those years there had been many strikes and layoffs. Since Vernon knew no other job, he always had to wait out each work stoppage. He picked up an odd job or two, but nothing that would help if the work stoppage lasted very long.

Then one did. It lasted over six months and left Vernon's savings account nearly empty. He decided then and there that he was going to learn a marketable skill and set up his own Weekend Wealth Venture.

Vernon enjoyed working with figures and, at the suggestion of a friend in the plant's personnel department, he began a night course in bookkeeping and accounting. In a short time, he had learned the basics and he started getting ready for income tax time which was coming up.

There were over 800 employees in Vernon's plant and between January and April 15 many of them came to him to have their tax returns prepared. Vernon did them on the weekends and often earned as much as $30 an hour.

Once the tax season was over, he contacted small businesses in town and soon had five sets of books that he took care of in his spare time—at $20 an hour. Vernon's Weekend Wealth Venture not only gave him the extra income he wanted, it also insured him of a steady income during work stoppages. Just as important, Vernon is confident of himself because he knows that he could quit his job at the mill anytime he wishes and operate his venture full-time. Vernon knows the satisfying feeling of security from a profitable Weekend Wealth Venture.

TURNING YOUR WEEKEND WEALTH VENTURE INTO A CHALLENGE

One of the greatest benefits your Weekend Wealth Venture can offer you is the satisfaction you can find by meeting a challenge and succeeding. A Weekend Wealth Venture can help you search for and find the type of work you prefer to do—and bring you extra money besides.

Your Weekend Wealth Venture can help you:

* Be your own boss - Take credit and profit from your ideas and your work.
* Discover your life's work - Expose yourself to many opportunities and methods until you find the right one for you and do it full-time.
* Do what you've always wanted to do - Give you the springboard and the confidence to move into the career that will make you happiest while offering you the profits you deserve.

How Natalie H. Discovered An Exciting Career With Her Weekend Wealth Venture

Natalie H. of Jackson, Tennessee, was bored stiff. For eight hours a day, five days a week, Natalie inspected intricate electronic circuits in a factory. The circuits seemed etched in her mind.

Natalie preferred to work with people and help them solve their problems. She was very outgoing and active in civic affairs. But Natalie felt that her job was holding her back both because of its dullness and because of the security it offered her in the form of a regular pay check. She felt she could not afford to give it up.

Finally, Natalie decided to try selling real estate on weekends—the busiest time. She quickly earned her agent's license and was soon working at a local real estate office Saturdays and Sundays. She loved it. Natalie was not only able to meet new people, she was also able to help them solve their housing problems. Natalie was very successful.

Since real estate agents aren't paid until the sale is completely closed—which often takes two months or more—Natalie didn't get her first check for awhile. Her patience soon paid off. Within six months Natalie was earning an extra $1,000 a month as a weekend real estate agent; and a year later she was making much more at her weekend job than at her weekday job. She quit the factory job and began working full-time at the job she enjoyed most—

selling real estate. Today Natalie is one of the most successful agents in Jackson because she used her Weekend Wealth
Venture to be her own boss, discover her life's work and do
what she's always wanted to do—profitably.

FINDING SUCCESS WITH YOUR WEEKEND WEALTH VENTURE

Everybody wants success in life. But what exactly is
success? Is it some distant and clouded destination? No,
actually success is a journey. Success is a day-to-day experience. Here's how to find success with your Weekend Wealth
Venture:

* *Set a goal* - Decide what you want to do with your
  time, your money and your life.
* *Work toward that goal* - Begin today planning the
  steps you will take to reach that goal; then begin with
  the first step.
* *Acknowledge your success* - As you complete each
  step in your goal remind yourself that you *are* a
  success—you are doing what you intended to do.

Let's meet another one of our over one hundred
Weekend Wealth Builders to illustrate how your Weekend
Wealth Venture can bring you the success you desire.

How Earl M. Gained Success In His Life

Earl M. came out of high school thinking he knew exactly what he wanted to do the rest of his life—he wanted to
drive trucks. Ten years and millions of miles later, Earl
discovered the feeling of success and enjoyment in trucking
was gone. In the mornings he drove a loaded semi from
Rochester to Albany, New York. In the afternoon he brought
another semi back. He did this five days a week.

Along the way, Earl had become friends with many
musicians who worked in the nightspots he frequented. He
envied them. Most were part-time musicians who worked in
the clubs for the money, the enjoyment and the chance of
becoming a success someday. Earl would have loved to join
them but he knew very little about music.

Earl had an idea. After talking it over with his musician friends he spent his days off booking engagements for bands throughout upstate New York. For ten percent of their bookings Earl would line up the engagements and handle the promotion of the band.

His income wasn't much at first, but soon Earl was earning over $100 a weekend with just a few phone calls. Just as important to Earl, he was succeeding. He helped many small bands and single musicians build their fame and eventually move on to the Catskills and even New York City. Each new booking was a success for Earl.

Today, Earl still drives a line-haul truck—but the miles are much smoother as he feels the personal satisfaction of success earned with his Weekend Wealth Venture.

ACTIVATING YOUR OWN WEEKEND WEALTH PLAN

It's time for *you* to move into action. Whether you are looking for a Weekend Wealth Venture that will bring you money, security, a challenge or success—or all of these things—it's time for you to decide on your destination and start moving toward it with your own Weekend Wealth Plan. It's time to set your goal.

A goal is nothing more than a place you want to be sometime in the future. If you were planning a trip, you would decide where you want to go, when you wanted to be there and whether you realistically could reach your destination with the time and resources you have.

Goals are set the same way. To be effective, a goal must be:

* *Specific* - It must give you an accurate idea of where you want to be.
* *Timed* - You must know approximately when you want to reach your goal in actual days, weeks, months or years.
* *Realistic* - It must be a goal that has been attained by others or is within the range of realistic human accomplishment.

To better illustrate how you can set your own Weekend Wealth Plan goal, let's see:

How Paul L. Established His Challenge Goal

More than anything, Paul L. of Mansfield, Ohio, wanted a challenge. He wanted to do something that was interesting and varied on the weekends while continuing to hold down his regular job as a teacher.

After carefully reviewing his interests and skills—as you will in the next chapter—Paul decided that he wanted to be a weekend auctioneer. That was Paul's Weekend Wealth Plan goal.

Paul made his goal specific: "I want to be a successful weekend auctioneer earning at least $250 extra each month."

Paul timed his goal: "I want to reach my goal within six months—by September."

Paul checked to make sure the goal was realistic: he talked with successful, working auctioneers who told him that he could sign up for a six-week auctioneer school course in a nearby state during the summer months when he was off from his teaching job. They further told him that there was a great need for apprentice auctioneers in the area and one offered to take him on as soon as he finished his course.

Paul's goal was specific, timed and realistic—and challenging. Today, Paul is a veteran auctioneer in Richland County, Ohio, because he set a goal—a destination—and moved toward it.

TAKING INVENTORY OF YOUR WEALTH BUILDING BLOCKS

To insure yourself of success with your Weekend Wealth Venture you must take an honest inventory of your Wealth Building Blocks—the assets you have that you can quickly turn into a profit. Here's how to find your own Wealth Building Blocks:

* *Review your past skills* - What skills do you have that you may not have used recently—ones that could easily be renewed? Typing? Welding? Sewing? Woodworking? Managing? Selling? Planning?
* *List your present skills* - What are your current skills that you use in your everyday job?
* *Set aside your time* - How much time do you have each week that you can spend on your Weekend Wealth Venture? One or two days off? Evening hours? Every other day? How many hours can you invest in your profit venture?

In the next chapter I'll show you exactly how to take inventory of your Wealth Building Blocks and discover the quickest way to Weekend Wealth. I'm giving you a quick preview of how you can find your own profit assets now because I want you to be thinking about them. I want your subconscious to begin helping you *right now* on the road to success with your Weekend Wealth Venture.

Dick And Darlene T. Built Big Profits With Their Wealth Building Blocks

Dick and Darlene T. of Clearwater, Florida, were looking for a Weekend Wealth Venture that they could operate together with their combined Wealth Building Blocks.

Together, they made a list of skills that they had shared in the past. All their children were grown and had moved away, and they had their greatest memories of the years when they raised their three boys and two girls. They topped their past skills list with "Good with children."

Darlene was a good cook and loved to entertain. She added this to their present skills list. Dick was an outgoing person who always found himself heading up the games at any parties they had. He wrote this down. The list went back and forth and Dick and Darlene added Wealth Building Blocks—individual and collective assets that they could use in their Weekend Wealth Venture.

Their final Block was a 48-hour block of time that they had available: Saturday and Sunday. Now came the question—what type of weekend opportunity could they develop using these Wealth Building Blocks?

Darlene thought of it first, shared it with Dick and they decided to do it. The T's now operate a very successful children's party service. Dick is the clown and Darlene makes and serves the cake. Since most kids' birthday parties are on weekends, Dick and Darlene can fit their Weekend Wealth Venture into their schedule. Charging from $25 to $75 a party, the T.'s often stage three to six parties a weekend and gross as much as $1,800 a month with few expenses. Dick and Darlene T. are successful Weekend Wealth Builders because they knew how to discover their own Wealth Building Blocks.

TRANSFORMING YOUR GOAL INTO A WEEKEND WEALTH PLAN

Once you have your goal in mind and you've taken a general look at your Wealth Building Blocks you must map out your own Weekend Wealth Plan and break it down into easy-to-reach steps.

To develop your own Weekend Wealth Plan you can ask yourself:

* Where am I today? How close am I right now to reaching my goal? Do I have all the skills and time I need? Will I have to gather more capital to start?
* Where do I want to be tomorrow? What will it take to reach my goal? What will I have when I reach my goal? More money? How much? Security? A challenge? Success?
* What's the quickest and easiest path between where I am and where I want to be? To reach my goal what must I do first? Second? Next? How long should each step in my Weekend Wealth Plan take to complete?

Linda D. Activated Her Own Weekend Wealth Plan Quickly

Linda D. knew right off what she wanted to do to earn extra money on weekends—she wanted to be an interior decorator. Linda trained as a decorator after leaving high school, but somehow got sidetracked into working as an executive secretary for six years. To move back into her old field on a full-time basis Linda decided to start working as a weekend interior decorator and gradually renew her skills. Here's how she did it.

Linda first asked herself, "Where am I today?" Her answer was, "a trained decorator with two days off a week and the need for experience."

Linda answered "Where do I want to be tomorrow?" with "I want to be a successful part-time, then full-time interior decorator within two years." That was Linda's goal.

Finally, Linda asked "What's the quickest and easiest path between where I am and where I want to be?" She answered, "Taking refresher courses in decorating, subscribing to decorating magazines to acquaint myself with the latest trends, and talking with local decorating studios about part-time work."

Linda's goal of becoming a successful interior decorator was now more than just a goal; it was a plan—a Weekend Wealth Plan. Today Linda has saved up enough money from her Weekend Wealth Venture to help her make the exciting change from a full-time executive secretary to a full-time decorator. Linda had a Plan.

ACTIVATING YOUR WEEKEND WEALTH PLAN FOR EXTRA CASH THIS WEEKEND

It's time to show you how you can activate your own Weekend Wealth Plan and add extra dollars to your pocket in your spare time. It's as easy as 1-2-3:

    1 - Decide on the first step you must take to reach your own Weekend Wealth Plan goal. It could be: contact potential customers, or order needed supplies, or draw a rough sketch of your design.

2 - Then decide what next steps you will need to take to bring you closer to your goal. They could include: set up a new checking account for your opportunity, see the bank about a small loan, decide on the best way to market your product or service, or apply for the job.

3 - Finally, take the first step toward your goal. Don't just plan it—do it. Make that first important step toward your goal that says "I plan to succeed." Don't stop until you've reached your goal.

Al S. Put His Weekend Wealth Plan Into Action

Al S. of Tucson, Arizona, had taken every step in the Weekend Wealth Plan. He set a specific, realistic and timely goal. He took inventory of his Wealth Building Blocks. He transformed his goal into a Weekend Wealth Plan with specific steps. He knew it was time to activate his plan and move toward success. Here's how he did it:

Al decided that his Weekend Wealth Venture was to be the buying and selling of used cars. Obviously, the first step toward reaching his plan was to *find profitable cars for sale.* The next steps were to *advertise his cars to potential buyers* and *sell his cars to the buyers and collect his profits.*

To activate his Weekend Wealth Venture, Al began scanning the newspaper and shopping center billboards for used car bargains. Al planned to sell the cars from his home rather than from an expensive lot and he would dress them up with a wax job and interior cleaning in his garage. By shopping around and calling all the ads, Al looked at nearly two dozen cars his first Saturday and bought two of them at very low prices. He cleaned them up the next day and put ads in the paper to sell them the following weekend.

Both cars were sold that second weekend—and Al earned a net profit of $345 on the two cars. Within six months, Al was selling three or four cars every weekend with two-day profits of as much as $1,000 cash. Not bad for a Weekend Wealth Venture. And it all happened because Al knew that planning is only part of success—*doing* is the most important part. Al activated his own profitable Weekend Wealth Plan.

HOW OTHER WEEKEND WEALTH BUILDERS HAVE FOUND SUCCESS WITH THEIR WEEKEND WEALTH PLAN

As you develop your own profitable opportunity, you may meet some of these successful Weekend Wealth Builders who have earned extra cash the easy way:

* Sam C. was looking for a Weekend Wealth Venture that was as much a challenge as a moneymaker. One of Sam's greatest building blocks was his fluent Spanish. By talking with a South American embassy employee, Sam was put in touch with four commercial firms in Costa Rica who needed a part-time representative in his home town of Los Angeles. It was easy work that offered good pay and—very important to Sam—a challenge.

* Mike W. enjoyed being active in civic affairs in his small Oregon town but he thought that no one would ever pay him for doing what he liked best—being involved. He was wrong. With my help he discovered that a nearby metropolitan newspaper was willing to pay him a regular salary for reporting on civic and social events in his town. They even showed him how to write them up. Mike enjoys his profitable Weekend Wealth Venture.

* Dorothy J. set her goal at earning an extra $500 a month with her Weekend Wealth Venture. With this in mind, Dorothy began looking around for a product she could easily make that had a high markup and little competition in her area. She decided on ceramics. After the purchase of a used kiln, her expenses were small—and her profits were soon big. Within three months, she surpassed her goal of $500 a month and has set a new goal of $750 a month working just two days a week.

* Bill E. decided he could make good money as a part-time coin trader. Once his goal was set, Bill planned his steps to success: buy coin pricing books and supplies, choose coins to sell from collections, sell and trade to members of a coin club, advertise in the club bulletin, attend local coin shows. Then Bill activated his plan and soon became a very successful coin trader with an income of as much as $200 a weekend. Bill is a successful Weekend Wealth Builder.

YOU CAN SUCCEED WITH YOUR OWN WEEKEND WEALTH PLAN

In this first chapter you've met one dozen successful Weekend Wealth Builders. There's nothing special about any of them—except that they have learned how to develop their own Weekend Wealth Plan. You can do the same.

You can succeed and bring in extra dollars with just a few hours and even fewer dollars invested. All you have to do is decide whether you want your Weekend Wealth Venture to bring you money or a challenge or both—then take the wide and well-traveled road to success mapped out by the many Weekend Wealth Builders you'll meet in this book.

You can join them—and turn your weekends into wealth.

ENERGIZING YOUR WEEKEND WEALTH PLAN

You're on your way to a more profitable and more enjoyable life with my Weekend Wealth Plan. Here's how *you* can turn the things you've learned in this chapter into stepping stones to Weekend Wealth *right now:*

1. Decide that you are going to cash in on your extra time and talents with your own Weekend Wealth Venture. Plan to follow the easy steps and clear illustrations in this book to your own satisfying goal. Start today!

2. Begin looking in your everyday life right now for a need that you can profitably fill for others. Open your eyes to the many possible opportunities for Weekend Wealth all around you. Carry a notebook to jot down ideas and observations.

3. Set your own Weekend Wealth goal right now. How much extra income are you looking for? How soon?

4. Make a simple list of the steps you'll probably need to take to reach your goal. What should you do first? Next? Then what? Plan your trip on paper and insure your own success.

5. Activate your Weekend Wealth Plan this week. Once you've decided what steps you need to take to reach your goal, take the first one and move ahead with your weekend opportunity.

6. Remind yourself: The road to Weekend Wealth is easy and well-traveled. My journey starts today.

Energizing Your Weekend Wealth Skills For Quick Profits

As a successful Weekend Wealth Builder, you must discover your own Wealth Building Blocks and learn how to turn them into quick, easy cash.

That's what this chapter is all about.

In the coming pages, you'll meet many more Weekend Wealth Builders who have traded their extra time and talents for the things they wanted from life: a new car, a larger home, more security, a better retirement. They know how easy it is to reach their own goals with my Weekend Wealth Plan.

You'll be able to follow their example—and learn from both their successes and failures. You see exactly how they take inventory of their time and skills—then turn these assets into profits in just a few hours a week. You'll soon join them as successful Weekend Wealth Builders and see your own dreams come true.

Let's get started!

HOW TO DISCOVER AND MARKET YOUR WEALTH BUILDING BLOCKS

As you learned in Chapter 1, Wealth Building Blocks are assets that you can quickly turn into cash. They include your past and present skills and one of your greatest assets—your valuable time. I'm going to show you exactly how to discover your own Wealth Building Blocks for yourself and also how to decide which ones will best take you to your goal and put money in your pocket quickly.

Then I'll show you how the smart Weekend Wealth Builders multiply their profits quickly and easily with advanced wealth-building techniques. You'll quickly zero in on your most profitable skills and make them available to the people who are most willing to pay you for them.

And, of course, each step of the way will be clearly illustrated by the many people just like yourself who wanted something more out of life and decided to go out and get it—the Weekend Wealth Builders.

PINPOINTING YOUR PROFITABLE TIME BLOCKS

Your most valuable Wealth Building Block is your *time*. Time belongs to both the person with the greatest success and the one with the poorest failure. They both are given 1,440 minutes each day. What they *do* with that time is what makes them different.

Here's how to find time to succeed with your own profitable Weekend Wealth Venture:

* *Write down your total available time* - For all of us it's the same: 168 hours or 10,080 minutes or 604,800 seconds a week.
* *Deduct time used for things more important than*

your *Weekend Wealth Venture* - Decide how much time you devote to your regular job, including commuting and lunch time, how much time for hobbies and relaxation, church and club activities, family time.

* *Add up the time you have available for your opportunity each week* - Subtract time used from time available.

* *Isolate valuable Time Blocks* - Move your duties around within your schedule to free up the largest blocks of time—such as on weekends or during evenings—for your Weekend Wealth Venture.

How Lee S. Discovered Valuable Time Blocks In A Very Busy Schedule

Lee S. of Wichita, Kansas, is like most of us: he didn't seem to have any extra time to do some of the things he wanted to—until he decided to rearrange his schedule by priority or *by the duty's importance to his goals.*

Let's see how he did it.

From his basic Time Block of 168 hours a week, Lee first deducted time needed to do the things that would bring himself and his family the food, shelter and security they needed. He deducted 56 hours for sleeping, another 55 hours for his job, commuting and lunch time, 8 hours for other meals, 10 hours a week for family time and another 10 hours for hobby, sports and relaxation. Just to be safe, Lee added 10% for flexibility. This gave Lee a total of about 153 hours a week—and left him with 15 hours a week to use in his Weekend Wealth Venture.

Once he deducted his used time from his available time, Lee decided to isolate those valuable 15 hours into Time Blocks that could be profitably used. He finally decided to use them in the form of two 7½-hour work days as a recycler. Lee set up a lucrative business picking up scrap steel, iron, other metals, paper, cardboard and other recycleable materials for resale. All he needed was time and his old pickup truck and Lee was soon earning as much as $80 a day with his Weekend Wealth Venture.

Three years later, Lee now has his teenaged son helping him with his business and Lee only works six hours on Saturday. Last year, Lee's recycling business netted him an extra $10,000—because he decided to put his time to good use with profitable Time Blocks.

UNCOVERING YOUR CURRENT SKILL BLOCKS—PROFITABLY

The easiest way to turn your time into quick cash is to market the skills you have right now. You have none? Look again. You have dozens of them—and here's how to find your most profitable Current Skill Blocks:

DYNAMIC SKILLS
Do you work well with people?
Do you enjoy helping others?
Can you help others feel comfortable?
Can you give clear directions?
Do others follow your lead?
Do you have many friends?
Do you make friends easily?
Can you help others learn?

POWER SKILLS
Do you know how to use common tools?
Can you use special tools?
Which ones?
Do you have a knack for building things?
Do you have a skill for fixing things?
Can you look at a rough sketch and visualize the complete product?

MIND SKILLS
Can you think about a problem for a while and find a solution?
Do you work with numbers easily?
Can you keep track of many things at once?
Are you always on the lookout for new and better ways of doing things?

How Steve D. Discovered His Own Current Skill Blocks And Turned Them Into A Profitable Weekend Wealth Venture

Steve D. lives in Van Nuys, California, one of the many cities within greater Los Angeles. Steve worked in the packaging department of a chair manufacturing firm—a job that required no special skills. I questioned him further to help him discover other current skills he might have that could be turned into weekend profits.

"Well, I do enjoy talking with people—and I am athletic and enjoy physical exercise," Steve told me.

"Okay," I said, "How about combining the two—what Weekend Wealth Ventures can we come up with using these two Current Skill Blocks?"

Here's part of the list we made up:

— Salesman in jogger's shop
— Salesman in sports shop
— Attendant in athletic club
— Market researcher

Steve asked, "What's a market researcher?" I explained and he decided that was the venture for him. Today, Steve walks door-to-door talking with people about their preferences in everything from dish soap to presidential candidates. He works on one of his two days off—Monday—and earns as much as $12 an hour talking with people and getting his exercise. Steve enjoys his Weekend Wealth Venture.

RETRIEVING PAST SKILL BLOCKS FOR QUICK CASH

You may find hundreds—even thousands—of dollars in easy money in skills you no longer use, but can quickly recondition. Don't overlook this great source of money-making skills. Ask yourself these questions:

* What job was I doing two years ago? Five years ago? Ten? Fifteen?

* What skills did I need to do these jobs? What Dynamic Skills did I use? Power Skills? Mind Skills?
* What will it take to sharpen these skills and turn them into cash again? Practice? Updating? Refresher courses? Books?
* Which of these Past Skill Blocks offers me the greatest potential for profit and success? Which one is next?

Chances are, within your past you have many good and useable skills that can quickly be dusted off and put back to work for you to bring you the money you desire with your Weekend Wealth Venture.

Give it a try.

How Leroy A. Built A Future With Past Skill Blocks

Leroy A. had a list of half a dozen Current Skill Blocks that could potentially bring him easy profits—but Leroy wanted more. He wanted a venture that would also be enjoyable.

Looking back, Leroy remembered enjoying most his four years as a bobtail truck driver. He liked the freedom of working alone while still being home for supper every evening. As the head of a shipping department, he rarely had the opportunity to get behind the wheel, and he missed it.

So Leroy decided to use his Past Skill Block—driving a truck—as the basis for his Weekend Wealth Venture.

With minimum capital, Leroy found that the best income would be gotten from starting a weekend hauling service in his hometown of Logan, Utah, a town of about 20,000. With an older pickup truck built up with plywood sides, Leroy offered to haul trash to the dump, help move families, deliver furniture or nursery stock—or anything that would bring him a profit.

Since starting his part-time business three years ago, Leroy has had to keep expanding to keep up with the demand. He's working at if full-time now and he has a much newer—and larger—truck. Best of all, Leroy's business brings him a net return of over *$500 a week*—and it all began with a Weekend Wealth Venture based on a Past Skill Block.

HOW TO APPRAISE SKILL BLOCKS FOR PROFIT

Once you've made a thorough list of both your Current and Past Skill Blocks—plus your valuable Time Block—you should decide which of these skills will take you to your goal most easily and profitably.

First, you have to review your own Weekend Wealth Plan goal. What is it? Money? Security? A challenge? Success? Two or more of these things?

Okay. Now write the number "1" next to the Skill Block that you would rate as the most profitable. Follow through and rate other skills "2," "3," and so on.

Next, rate your Skill Blocks by enjoyment. After all, part of the reason you've looking for a Weekend Wealth Venture is probably to get a change of pace from your regular job. Letter your skills "A," "B," "C" and so on by their importance to you.

Finally, begin matching up the most obvious skills on a separate piece of paper. If you have a Skill Block that's rated "1-A" list it first. Others should follow by their ratings.

Now you're ready to think about how to use these skills profitably—and you will as soon as you see how another Weekend Wealth Builder became her own part-time boss.

Jan R. Combined Current And Past Skill Blocks Successfully

Jan R. of Columbia, Missouri, had a conflict. Using my Skill Block Rating System, Jan rated "Oil Painting" as an "A" in enjoyable skills and "Selling Paintings" as a "1" under profitable skills. The conflict arose because Jan rated "Selling my own Oil Paintings" as a number "9"—very low on her scale. She enjoyed selling paintings but she realized that she needed more training before she could become a highly profitable painter herself.

Once she looked at the problem, the solution came easily. Jan decided to sell not only her own works but also the works of other local artists who had more experience and training.

It worked. Jan now operates "Floating Gallery"—a selection of original paintings by local artists that are displayed in public buildings throughout Columbia and Jefferson City, Missouri. Jan charges her artists a 15 percent commission on sold paintings and offers them wide exposure in return. Since Wednesday is Jan's day off as a nurse, she used that day to move paintings around among her many showplaces—and to collect her money for paintings sold.

As an art broker, Jan is able to not only turn her spare time into quick and easy cash, she's also able to pinpoint what local art buyers want and can aim her own "Oil Painting" Skill Block at the ready market. Jan now sells her paintings of local historical buildings for very impressive prices. This income, combined with her lucrative art dealership business, offers Jan Weekend Wealth *and* enjoyment.

TURNING YOUR SKILL BLOCKS INTO WEEKEND WEALTH

Using my Weekend Wealth Plan, you've discovered many profitable Skill Blocks and your valuable Time Block. It's time to turn these assets into spendable cash in the shortest time. Here's how to develop your Skill Blocks:

* *Profitable Experience* - One of the best ways to renew or build your Skill Blocks is to gain additional experience in using them either through a job that uses these skills or through practice.
* *Wealth Building Books* - You can also hone your Skill Blocks by learning from other people's experience through books such as this one and specific books on your skills.
* *Crash Courses* - Another method of trading time for improved Skill Blocks is to sign up for evening or weekly classes. You can probably find a crash course

to help you develop your Skill Blocks close to your own home.

How Christie L. Sharpened Her Skill Blocks And Turned Them Into Easy Cash

Christie L. of Austin, Minnesota, decided to build her Weekend Wealth with a profitable cooking school. She not only enjoyed cooking, but she also found pleasure in teaching others to develop their cooking skills.

To develop her own Skill Blocks, Christie began using my Weekend Wealth Plan to increase her income potential. First, she enrolled in an evening class in advanced cooking to both refresh her skills and learn new techniques.

Next, Christie took a part-time job as a salad chef in an Austin restaurant to gain experience and to watch the head chef who had an international reputation.

Then she began supplementing her collection of cook books with current ones that would help her in her classes.

Finally, Christie set a target date and began preparing for the first day of her cooking school in her home.

Aided by a feature in the local newspaper, Christie soon built up her enrollment to 15 students in her once-a-week class that Christie held on her day off from her regular job. At ten dollars per student per week—and with few costs—Christie was making a full $150 a week in extra money with her three-hour-a-week class. She offered the class' culinary results to a nearby rehabilitation center at cost. Her cooking school not only helped her and her students—it also offered eating pleasure to others.

Christie's cooking school was a success!

GENERATING ROUND HOLES FOR ROUND PEGS

As you discover and develop your Weekend Wealth Skill Blocks, you can also find new and profitable applications for your skills with the Weekend Wealth Plan. Here's how:

* Ask yourself: What are others doing with these same skills? Have I seen or heard of other Weekend Wealth

Builders who have applied these same Skill Blocks profitably? How did they do it?

* Ask yourself: How can I adapt these Skill Blocks to new opportunities? What would be the most logical use for these Skill Blocks? What unique uses could they be put to?
* Ask yourself: How can I quickly turn these Skill Blocks—individually and collectively—into quick cash? Is there a missing key or missing skill that will help me develop my Weekend Wealth?

By reviewing your Skill Blocks as you learn about new and profitable applications of the Weekend Wealth Plan, you can develop new and unique opportunities for building extra income in your spare time.

How Gary M. Discovered New Weekend Wealth Ventures

Gary M. of Saginaw, Michigan, had a problem. Gary's main Skill Block was "music." He played a number of instruments well. The problem was that Gary worked the swing shift in a local mill and wouldn't be able to take advantage of the most obvious opportunity for him— working as a part-time musician.

Gary gave the problem some thought. He began looking for another profitable Weekend Wealth Venture that he could develop during the day with his musical talents. He asked himself:

* What are others doing with these skills?
* How can I adapt these Skill Blocks to new opportunities?
* How can I turn these Skill Blocks into quick cash?

The answer came to Gary as he scanned the Saginaw phone book. Under "Music" in the Yellow Pages he found:

Music-Background
Music Instruction
Music-Sheet & Book
Musical Instruments-Dealers
Musical Instruments-Rentals
and others

That was it! Gary decided to use two hours each day—instead of his weekend days off—to teach music to students. He also planned to invest a few hundred dollars in musical instruments and rent them to his students. Today, Gary has built his small Weekend Wealth Venture into a highly profitable music studio that he operates full-time. Last year, Gary paid taxes on a net profit of $38,000. Gary now knows how to find new and profitable opportunities for his Skill Blocks.

And so do you.

SETTING THE BOUNDARIES ON YOUR WEEKEND WEALTH VENTURE LOCATION

One of the few limitations you will have to place on your profitable Weekend Wealth Venture is its location. That is, if your full-time job is located in Indianapolis, Indiana, you won't be able to build your venture in Portland, Oregon.

This limitation on you—and your customers—can be easily overcome by operating through the mails or by telephone. Of course, if your Weekend Wealth Venture is one where you must go to your customers or they must come to you you'll have to draw a line around you to mark off where you can practically operate your venture.

To draw this boundary, you simply have to take out a map of your area, mark off the location of your home, the location of your regular job, and the location of the majority of your customers. Here's an example:

How Terry L. Set Up His Weekend Wealth Venture Boundary —And Used It To Discover A New Opportunity

Terry L. was seemingly limited in Weekend Wealth opportunities by the size of his hometown, Mt. Ayr, Iowa, population 1,800. Even so, Terry planned to remain in the small town and build his income with a profitable Weekend Wealth Venture—if he could find one.

He decided against ventures that were operated by phone or the mails because he wanted to meet his customers in person. Terry decided that he would find a venture where his customers came to him; so he took out a map of his area and drew a circle around it marking out 25 miles in all directions. Then he sat down to think about what people in this area wanted enough to come to him to buy.

Terry decided that what most of these people in his area had in common was that they all made a living from the soil—they were farmers and ranchers, or suppliers to farmers and ranchers. Terry owned only a few acres near town, so he decided he would probably have to be a supplier rather than a farmer.

Finally, Terry drew up a list of Weekend Wealth Ventures that might be profitable in his area. From them, he chose a fencing service. Terry would use his pickup truck to haul fencing and posts from farm to farm and offer to put up new fencing or repair old fencing at a profitable per-foot rate. Farmers in the area, who were usually short-handed except during harvest, welcomed help with fence mending. After hours at his regular job in Mt. Ayr, and during his days off, Terry built up a very lucrative Weekend Wealth Venture by drawing a boundary and deciding what service he could profitably offer the people within it.

Terry is a smart Weekend Wealth Builder.

ENJOYING YOUR WEEKEND WEALTH VENTURE WHILE YOU MAKE BIG PROFITS

Of course, one of the reasons for discovering your own unique Weekend Wealth Venture is to offer you a challenge and success at something you can enjoy. So let's set aside the money aspect for a moment and help you discover a Weekend Wealth Venture that will add more fun to your life.

To do so, ask yourself:

* What have I done in the past that I've really enjoyed doing?
* What hobbies have I had that gave me pleasure?
* Are there tasks that I've performed in old jobs that I found enjoyable?
* Are there tasks in my current job that I especially like to do?

* What do I do for recreation? Collect? Build? Read? Travel?
* What jobs have I seen others perform that I thought would be enjoyable?

Then ask yourself:

* Okay. Now, of these pleasant tasks, which could be built into a profitable Weekend Wealth Venture?

How Barry R. Built A Weekend Wealth Venture That He Enjoyed

Barry R. made a comprehensive list of profitable part-time opportunities available in his area, but nothing struck his interest. Barry was looking for something that he could do that would not only be profitable, but fun as well.

Through self-inventory, Barry discovered that his Dynamic Skill Blocks were strong and that his job as a fireman gave him every other day off. Then Barry made a list of things he would enjoy doing for money:

- Working in a circus
- Buying and selling antiques
- Being a comedian
- Being a clown
- Selling things to people in the park or zoo
- Repairing model railroads

Such a diverse list of enjoyable ventures gave Barry many profitable ideas. By combining a couple of them, Barry found one that he felt would bring him both enjoyment and profits: dressing as a clown and selling balloons to children in the park or at the zoo. After renting a clown costume for a few days, buying the balloons and a tank of helium, and selling balloons in the park, Barry soon discovered that this was the type of Weekend Wealth Venture he was looking for. He found that his profits on a typical day were $75 to $100 and more. Just as important to Barry, he found a challenging venture that offered him a break from his regular job and the chance to put on a happy face for others.

A successful Weekend Wealth Builder doesn't make his choice of ventures based only on profits. He also considers opportunities that will bring him enjoyment. By being creative, the smart Wealth Builder can find both.

HOW OTHER WEEKEND WEALTH BUILDERS HAVE DISCOVERED AND MARKETED THEIR WEALTH BUILDING BLOCKS

Thousands of other smart people have overcome small obstacles on their road to enjoyment and profits with my Weekend Wealth Plan. Here are a few more:

* Walter L. used my self-inventory methods to discover that he had many things to offer others profitably. Along with two days off each week, Walter had both Dynamic and Power Skills. He could work easily with both things and people. Using his pickup truck, Walter developed a very profitable Weekend Wealth Venture: he sold seasonal fruits and vegetables at a roadside stand. He would purchase watermelons, grapes, corn or other produce in quantity from nearby farmers, and set up his stand in the back of his pickup truck. He would then park in a busy shopping center. On many weekends, Walter made $200 or more from his Weekend Wealth Venture.

* Harold K. worked the swing shift at a furniture factory in Lenoir, North Carolina. He quickly discovered a need in his area for a small janitorial service for area businesses, and he set one up. He would load his cleaning supplies in his car and handle janitorial jobs in an hour or two on his way home from work after midnight. Harold's Weekend Wealth Venture offered him an extra $500 in easy money each month—and still gave him his weekends. He's a smart Weekend Wealth Builder.

YOU CAN SUCCEED WITH WEALTH BUILDING BLOCKS

At this moment, you have all the things you need to begin building a profitable and enjoyable Weekend Wealth Venture. You have your Wealth Building Blocks.

You've learned how to discover and take inventory of your Time Blocks, your Dynamic Skills, Power Skills and Mind Skills profitably.

You've also learned how to develop and market these valuable Wealth Building Blocks as you discover your own unique application of my Weekend Wealth Plan.

Along the way you've been introduced to 22 successful Weekend Wealth Builders—and dozens more are waiting—to help you find your own successful venture.

You're definitely on your way to success, extra cash, and satisfaction with your own profitable Weekend Wealth Venture.

ENERGIZING YOUR WEEKEND WEALTH PLAN

It's time to put what you've learned in this chapter into action! Here are some things *you* can do *right now* to begin adding extra profits and satisfaction to your life with a Weekend Wealth Venture:

1. Discover your own unique Wealth Building Blocks. Take an inventory of your profitable Time Blocks and think about how you can use them as a smart Weekend Wealth Builder.

2. Uncover your current and past Skill Blocks. Review the skills you've developed in your life thus far and write them down. Leave none of them out—all of them are important and potentially profitable.

3. Decide how you can sharpen your most profitable and enjoyable Skill Blocks through books, courses and additional experience. Improve your inventory of Skill Blocks with suggestions in this chapter.

4. Mark out your Weekend Wealth Plan Boundary and decide where your customers live and what needs they want fulfilled.

5. Make sure that the Weekend Wealth Ventures you're developing are ones that you will enjoy doing. Have fun while you make money in your spare time.

3

How Weekend Wealth Builders Create Dynamic Profit Ventures Fast

You're on your way to Weekend Wealth!

You've discovered your own unique Wealth Building Blocks—valuable time and skills that you can quickly turn into spendable cash. You've chosen the most enjoyable and most profitable of these and decided to put them to work for you in your own Weekend Wealth Venture.

Now it's time to expose yourself to as many of the creative Weekend Wealth Ventures as you can, and make the decision of activating the one that will take you to your own personal goals.

In this chapter I'm going to show you how you can discover hundreds of new Weekend Wealth Ventures all around you right now. From them you can choose the right one for you. You'll soon see profitable Weekend Wealth Ventures everywhere you look—home, job, hobbies, recreation and more—and learn how to zero in on the best and most profitable ones quickly and easily.

Let't get going!

GATHERING AND ANALYZING PROFITABLE WEEKEND WEALTH VENTURES

In the coming pages you're going to learn how smart Weekend Wealth Builders find potentially profitable weekend business opportunities. You'll discover the basic types of opportunities available to you, and how and where to come up with hundreds—even thousands—of successful Weekend Wealth Ventures.

Then you'll learn how to save yourself valuable time and money by analyzing your opportunity to make sure it is not only a profitable and workable venture, but also one that will take you to your own personal goals in a short time.

Here's just a hint of what you'll learn:

* How to quickly analyze the market for your potential ventures before you spend any money on developing them for profit.
* How to beat your competition at its own game and multiply your profits.
* How to estimate your potential income from your chosen Weekend Wealth Ventures.
* How to analyze your expenses and discover hidden profits *before* you put your Weekend Wealth Venture into action.
* How other successful Weekend Wealth Builders have used these profitable techniques to add dollars to their pockets in their spare time.

A smart Weekend Wealth Builder earns his money on paper and—if he's satisfied with the return—turns his venture into easy cash.

LOCATING THE PERFECT WEEKEND WEALTH VENTURE FOR YOU

If there were only a half dozen or so successful and profitable Weekend Wealth opportunities, you would have little choice and would have to modify your Time Blocks and Skill Blocks to fit them. Thankfully, it isn't that way. This book offers more than one hundred opportunities and this chapter will show you how to discover ten times more.

Even so, there are actually only three types of business opportunities and every Weekend Wealth Venture can be classified as one of them. Here they are:

* *Manufacturing* - is a broad group of opportunities where raw materials are turned into a finished product. In the timber industry, the raw material is trees and the finished product is lumber. In home construction, the raw material is lumber and the finished product is houses. Thousands of Weekend Wealth Builders make their profits in one or two days a week manufacturing needed products.

* *Distribution* - Once the product is made, it must somehow reach the consumer. This is where distributors come in and make their profits. They buy at wholesale prices from the manufacturer and sell at retail prices to the consumer. Hundreds of profitable weekend opportunities are available in this necessary field.

* *Services* - Sometimes the product sold is intangible and unseen. Service opportunities combine time and skills profitably. Typical services offered by Weekend Wealth Builders include research service, landscaping service, TV repair service, tutoring, collection service and hundreds of others. Since little or no inventory is needed to start a service venture, this is often the easiest to get into and often the most profitable.

To give you a better picture of how a smart Weekend Wealth Builder can discover the right opportunity from among these three types, let's see:

How Larry W. Turned A Misfortune Into A Fortune

If you live in Springfield, Oregon, you may know Larry W. You might even have known him a few years ago when he was having financial problems and the money from his regular job as an office manager wasn't enough to cover his expenses.

In fact, Larry's bank was ready to repossess his car and furniture before he finally woke up to the Weekend Wealth Plan.

In just one evening, Larry turned it all around. Here's how: first, he analyzed his own Time Blocks and Skill Blocks. With two days off each week—Monday and Tuesday—Larry began looking for a Weekend Wealth Venture in which he could use his training and experience in office procedures for quick profits. With the three basic types of opportunities in mind, Larry listed these applications:

Manufacturing	Make small office equipment
	Make desk sets or name plaques
	Make literature racks or trays
Distribution	Sell office supplies
	Sell bookkeeping equipment and supplies
	Start a mail order supplies venture
Services	Start an office employment agency
	Become an office procedures consultant
	Teach office practices at night school

Then Larry chose the Weekend Wealth Venture that best fit his financial and interest needs. Today, Larry W. offers a part-time office procedures consulting service in the Eugene-Springfield area and is considering expanding it to full-time. After all, he's earning $20 an hour and more. Many months he doubles up on his mortgage payment and his car is completely paid for. The bank is much friendlier to him now.

Larry chose a profitable Weekend Wealth Venture from among the three types of business opportunities.

USING YOUR OBSERVATION SKILLS
TO TURN UP PROFITABLE VENTURES

You and I are in the middle of a pretty big world of opportunity. Around us are literally thousands of people who wish us to buy something from them. If we can look at them objectively and with an open mind, we can discover hundreds of ideas that offer us Weekend Wealth.

Here's how you can open your eyes to profit opportunities around you right now:

* Shelter opportunities - Look for creative needs you have all around you—in your home, garage, yard, kitchen, car and other places where the average person would want something to make his life easier or more enjoyable.

* Social opportunities - The people in your life all have needs and desires that you can fulfill profitably. Talk with friends, relatives, co-workers, acquaintances and others about what products and services they would like to see made available.

* Work opportunities - Many successful Weekend Wealth Builders find their profitable opportunities as near as their regular job. They discover a related product or service with built-in customers. They supply needed items to their employers. They find many ventures on the job.

The smart Weekend Wealth Builder opens his eyes and his mind to the world around him because he knows that there are hundreds of profitable spare time opportunities to be found in his own life.

How Joe C. Used His Observation Skills To Build Weekend Wealth

Joe C. of Provo, Utah, is a house painter by trade. Being conscious of the things that are or are not painted, Joe found the perfect Weekend Wealth Venture for him. Here's how it happened:

Joe was pulling into a Provo supermarket parking lot one day a couple of years ago, and he noticed how many of the cars were parked crooked and that many valuable parking spaces were wasted. He could easily see the cause: the parking lot stripes had been worn away with time and weather. Maybe he could paint them on his day off.

Inside the market, Joe asked to see the manager and walked out with him to the parking lot to show him the waste of parking space. Then Joe told him he was a professional painter and that he would repaint the stripes at a reasonable price. The manager quickly approved the work and Joe agreed to start the following Saturday morning before the store opened.

In the meantime, Joe checked into striping equipment and found a large rental agency that had parking lot stripers for rent by the day. He signed up for one.

Then Joe talked to other market, restaurant and shopping center owners in the area and lined up two more customers that first weekend.

Today Joe adds an extra $300 to $600 a month to his income as a house painter by painting parking lot stripes on one of his days off each week. Joe learned that—by opening your eyes and your mind to the many opportunities around you—a smart Weekend Wealth Builder can see profits all around him.

So can you!

UNCOVERING PROFITABLE WEEKEND WEALTH VENTURES IN BOOKS

The greatest friends you'll find on your way to Weekend Wealth are books. Books can offer in a short time the valuable ideas of many people and many years. In books you can meet people much like yourself who strive for a better life and have found it. They give you ideas and clear steps on how you can succeed. The smart Weekend Wealth Builder relies heavily on books to give him worthwhile business ideas plus information on how he can make his life and his work more productive.

Here's how you can discover books that will help you on your road to success as a Weekend Wealth Builder:

* Bookstores - Check your local phone book and nearby shopping centers for bookstores. Ask for business and self-help books. You can discover dozens of titles that will not only cut time off your search for wealth, but also enlarge the opportunities you seek.
* Used bookstores - are also an excellent source of valuable books on subjects of value to the Weekend Wealth Builder.
* Mail order books - There are hundreds of worthwhile books available to you through mail order companies. The largest is the publisher of this book, Parker Publishing Company, Inc., West Nyack, N.Y. 10994. Write for their current catalog of business opportunity books.
* Libraries - Your local library may have some of the books you need. The library also offers you an opportunity to discover worthwhile books that you can later buy from bookstores for your own success library.
* Friends - Talk with friends about your interest in business opportunity and self-help books. They may be able to recommend a favorite title to you.
* Newspaper review columns - Watch your local newspaper—especially a metropolitan daily newspaper—for book reviews and ads for upcoming books that can help you on your road to success.

Virgil D. Found His Weekend Wealth Venture In My Book

Virgil D. of Muncie, Indiana, related this story to me recently. He had been trying to decide how he could build a small part-time business at home, with little luck. He came up with a short list of opportunities, but none appealed to him enough to spur him on.

Then one day, Virgil was waiting for his wife who was shopping in a shopping center, when he passed a chain bookstore. Out of curiosity he walked in and asked for books about small business opportunities. On the shelves he discovered my book, *How to Earn Over $50,000 a Year at Home*, and opened it up.

A half hour later, Virgil's wife found him in the bookstore still scanning my book. He had found more than a half-dozen opportunities that he was interested in developing profitably. He bought the book and took it home to read.

Today, Virgil operates a profitable retail business in his spare time and earns $100 a week and more. He discovered this opportunity—and the steps to making it succeed—in my book. I'm proud to be able to relate this story to you and illustrate the value of books to the smart Weekend Wealth Builder.

DISCOVERING HUNDREDS OF NEW WEEKEND WEALTH VENTURES THAT CAN BRING YOU QUICK PROFITS

To succeed as a Weekend Wealth Builder and discover the perfect opportunity, you must expose yourself to as many Weekend Wealth Ventures as you can. Here are some valuable sources for hundreds of profitable opportunities all around you:

* The Yellow Pages - The telephone business directory lists hundreds and even thousands of successful business ventures, many of which can be converted into profitable Weekend Wealth Ventures. The telephone company or local library will have Yellow Pages from many metropolitan areas that can offer you new ways to wealth.

* Newspaper ads - Many smart Weekend Wealth Builders rely on local and out-of-state newspapers to offer them new business opportunities. Displays and

classified ads merchandise new products, new services and new techniques for reaching your customers.

* Small Business Administration - The SBA is designed to serve people just like you who wish to take advantage of our economic system's benefits. The SBA offers counseling, financial assistance, management ideas, books, pamphlets, statistics and other information worthwhile to the Weekend Wealth Builder. You can receive a copy of their publications list and field offices by writing to the Small Business Administration, 450 Golden Gate, San Francisco, CA 94102.

How Ellen S. Discovered The Right Weekend Wealth Venture In An Alternate Venture Source

Ellen S. of San Angelo, Texas, worked in a typing pool in a government office. She enjoyed typing and her speed was 80 to 90 words a minute. Her Skill Blocks included a good command of English and the ability to work with people. Here's how she turned her skills into spare time cash:

Ellen picked up the Ft. Worth telephone book and looked up "Typing Service." She found ads for typists who worked both out of their homes and from a commercial office. Since this was a part-time venture, Ellen decided to operate from her home.

But Ellen wanted to do something more unique and challenging than what she did at her regular job—she wanted a different typing venture. She found it in the Yellow Pages at the end of the "Typing Service" listings. It read: "See also: Manuscript Typing." She did, and found a handful of typists who specialized in retyping manuscripts for writers.

Since she wouldn't be competing with them, Ellen called ed three of the manuscript typists in Ft. Worth, over 200 miles away. They offered her ideas on how to start her venture and what to charge. One also sent Ellen a sample of how to type manuscripts for writers and editors. She was on her way.

Today, Ellen operates a successful spare time moneymaker from her home: a manuscript typing service that nets her over $500 extra dollars a month because she let her mind do the thinking in the Yellow Pages.

ANALYZING YOUR WEEKEND WEALTH VENTURES SUCCESSFULLY

By now you probably have three or four solid Weekend Wealth Venture opportunities in mind and you're ready to choose the best and most profitable one and turn it into quick and easy cash in your spare time. Here's how the successful Weekend Wealth Builders do it:

* *First: Identify Need* - With each of your part-time ventures, decide what it is your potential customer is looking for. What need does he have? How can you best fill it profitably?
* *Then: Identify Customers* - Who will be buying your product or service? Older women, young housewives, breadwinners, children, dog owners or car drivers? Do this for each of your opportunities.
* *Finally: Estimate Market Size* - How many customers are there for your products and services? One hundred? One thousand? One million? Will they be one-time or repeat customers?

How Ralph J. Analyzes His Profit Market

Ralph J. of Red Bluff, California, enjoyed working with tools and making things. He finally chose a weekend key shop as his Weekend Wealth Venture. To make sure it would be a needed and profitable business, Ralph reviewed the three steps to choosing the right opportunity:

Need - Ralph discovered that there is not only a strong need for keymakers throughout the United States but that there was also a specific need in his community. There were few in the Red Bluff phone book.

Customer - Ralph found out that his potential customers are a cross-section of society: homeowners, apartment dwellers, car owners, warehouse owners, real estate agents and others. Since other areas were covered by key shops, Ralph decided that the majority of his customers would live on the east side of town.

Quantity - There were thousands of customers in this area who had to get keys made a great distance from their homes. Ralph knew that they would welcome his business as a convenience and become repeat customers.

As an extra feature, Ralph decided that, rather than rent a key shop or use his garage for the part-time enterprise, he would build a box on his pickup truck and take his business to the people. On Saturday morning he would park at one location and move to another in the afternoon. He was also on call Sundays for lockwork when all the other shops in town were closed.

Ralph discovered and analyzed a very profitable Weekend Wealth Venture with this three-step plan for discovering the market for any business opportunity.

THE FOUR-STEP SYSTEM FOR
NEUTRALIZING COMPETITION

How would you like to quickly analyze and overcome competition to your Weekend Wealth Venture and add thousands of extra profit dollars to your bank account? You can—with my successful four-step system used by smart Weekend Wealth Builders:

* *Identify Your Competitors* - Whom will you be competing with in each of your potential Weekend Wealth Ventures? Where are they located? What area do they serve?
* *Estimate Their Effectiveness* - How well are they serving their market? Are they a prosperous and profitable venture? Can you estimate their profits?
* *Discover Their Weak Points* - How could they improve their market service and profit picture? Are they managed well? Could a smaller, more personal venture draw some of their customers away successfully? How much is their gross income? Profit?

* *Decide How To Counteract Your Competitor* - What can you offer potential customers that will make your product or service more special than that of your competitor and thus earn additional business? Can you offer a broader venture? More specialized venture? An easier to use business?

Now let's watch this four-step system in action with a successful Weekend Wealth Builder.

How Carl A. Joined His Competitor And Multiplied His Profits

Carl A. developed a Weekend Wealth Venture that was not only profitable, but was also enjoyable: he raised tropical fish.

Carl's problem was that he had hit his growth limit because he was in direct competition with an older and larger fish supplier in his town of Denver, Colorado, and had difficulty competing with the supplier's price and selection—until he decided to neutralize the competition between the two.

Carl decided that, rather than run in direct competition to the major supplier, he would specialize in a specific type of tropical fish and sell them to this and other suppliers for less than they could raise them for themselves. He chose betas and, after talking with his future customers, began building his modified Weekend Wealth Venture at home. Soon he was supplying most of the betas in Colorado and Utah through his wholesalers. He had no competition. Today Carl operates his tropical fish supply house—*The Beta Shack*—full-time and earns more than he did before he decided to neutralize competition.

PINPOINTING PROFITS WITH YOUR WEEKEND WEALTH VENTURE

To make the best decision on which of the many opportunities you've discovered should be turned into a profitable Weekend Wealth Venture, you must decide which will be the most profitable for you. Here's how smart Wealth Builders estimate potential income and expenses from their enterprises:

* *Estimate Potential Users* - How many customers can you find for your product or service? Can you reach them and sell them quickly and easily?
* *Estimate Sales Per User* - Will your customers buy from you once? Twice? A dozen times? Is your product or service a once-in-a-lifetime purchase or one that must be repurchased frequently?
* *Estimate Sales Price* - What price will you set for your product or service?
* *Estimate Total Income Potential* - Multiply the sales price by the number of units you expect to sell in one year. This is your estimated total yearly income.
* *Estimate Start-Up Capital Needed, If Any* - How much cash do you need to start your Weekend Wealth Venture?
* *Estimate Operating Costs To Offer Your Venture* - How much will it cost to run your enterprise on a day-to-day basis? Will you have to hire outside labor? How much is your own time worth as owner and chief laborer?
* *Estimate Total Expenses* - Decide how much your product or service will cost to produce by estimating labor, overhead and raw materials cost and adding it to your capital investment.
* *Estimate Profits* - Finally, subtract your estimated total expenses from your estimated total income for each Weekend Wealth Venture you are considering. How much is this per year? How much per unit sold or service rendered?

How Fred E. Found His Most Profitable Weekend Wealth Venture

Fred E. of Lewiston, Idaho, chose operating a part-time popcorn stand over three other Weekend Wealth Ventures because of the high profits he found in it.

Fred decided he would operate his popcorn stand near the local Little League field on Saturdays and at a large metropolitan park on Sunday afternoons. This gave him a large group of potential customers—many of whom would buy more than one bag each weekend. He decided that, based on the price of popcorn at amusement parks and other places in his area, he could get 35 cents and 50 cents for his bags of popcorn.

Fred estimated that his setup would initially cost him about 200 dollars for the popcorn machine and a cart if he built and painted the cart himself and he bought the machine used. He spread the cost over a two-year period, planning to buy a new one at that time if the enterprise was successful.

Then Fred estimated costs: by counting heads at the field and park and estimating that one out of ten would probably buy a bag from him, Fred expected to sell about 400 bags in a weekend. He estimated his costs at 18 cents and 23 cents a bag including labor and overhead. That gave him a 100 percent markup—and an estimated profit of 200 dollars a weekend.

Based on this estimate, Fred decided to set up his popcorn wagon and begin his Weekend Wealth Venture. In practice, Fred found that his estimates of income and expenses were close. Popcorn sales ranged from 250 to 500 bags per weekend depending on the weather and other factors.

Three years later, Fred's popcorn wagon is still a profitable Weekend Wealth Venture—for his 15-year-old son who is saving up his part of the profits for college. Fred spends his time watching the Little League games as he makes money from his part-time enterprise.

Fred is a smart Weekend Wealth Builder who knows how to estimate income and expenses before starting his new venture.

HOW OTHER SUCCESSFUL WEEKEND WEALTH BUILDERS FIND AND ANALYZE PROFITABLE VENTURES

Here are a few more successful spare time operators who turn Time and Skill Blocks into extra profits. Their experiences may be the key you need on your road to extra cash in a hurry:

* Stan O. enjoyed music, but didn't want to spend his spare time teaching children how to read and play music. So he made a list of other things he could do with his skill and time and came up with a half-dozen profit venture ideas. He chose the best one for him: playing music with a local group in area night clubs. Stan now has his own group and earns an extra $750 a month doing something he enjoys.

* Claudia D. enjoyed making handicrafts, but really didn't like the selling part. She just didn't want to sit in a booth at the flea market all day and wait for customers to buy from her. Using my Weekend Wealth Building Techniques, she decided to let others do the selling for her. She offered her crafts to others who had booths, on a consignment basis. That is, if they sold her crafts they could give her the wholesale price and keep a profit for themselves. Of course, Claudia's wholesale price allowed a healthy profit for herself while she did other things with her weekend.

YOU CAN DISCOVER AND DEVELOP YOUR OWN WEEKEND WEALTH VENTURE

There are literally hundreds of potentially successful Weekend Wealth Ventures around you at this moment—and they're there to produce quick, easy cash if you take advantage of them.

You now know that there are many types of successful part-time opportunities available to you—plus, you know exactly how to find new ones any time you wish.

You also know how to quickly analyze each and every opportunity you come in contact with for profitability. You know how to analyze the market, beat the competition, and estimate your potential income, expenses and profits.

Just as important, you've seen nine more successful Weekend Wealth Builders in action who know how to turn ideas into cash with my Weekend Wealth Plan.

ENERGIZING YOUR WEEKEND WEALTH PLAN

Let's move into action. Here's how to start making extra cash *right now* with what you've learned in this chapter about finding and analyzing profitable opportunities:

1. Begin a Potential Profit List of Weekend Venture opportunities you feel you should consider. List a few from each of three categories: manufacturing, distribution and services.

2. Open your eyes to the profitable ventures all around you. Watch for basic needs and profit opportunities in your home, at work and among friends and social contacts. Keep a list of the best ideas.

3. Watch for new and unique wealth opportunities in your Profit Library. Review the more than 100 successful ventures in this book—plus other opportunity books you can find—for the right one for you.

4. Turn on your creative powers as you review other sources of part-time opportunities: the telephone book, newspaper ads, Small Business Administration and others. Any one of these sources can be worth thousands of dollars in extra profits.

5. Analyze your Weekend Wealth Venture successfully by identifying a need, a customer for it, the number

of potential customers, the income potential, expenses and profits from the venture.

6. Neutralize competition with my four-step system of identifying and improving on the products and services your competitors are offering. Earn their customers and add many thousands of dollars in extra profits to your pocket.

Ten New Methods
For Activating Your
Weekend Wealth
Venture With
No-Risk Capital

"It takes money to make money!"

That isn't necessarily true! Thousands of smart Weekend Wealth Builders have started with little or no capital and built up impressive part-time profits with little more than a good idea. Others have opened up a world of extra cash with Rented Money.

So can you! In this chapter you'll learn how to start your Weekend Wealth Venture with little or none of your own money—plus how to cut the chances of loss to nearly zero percent.

You're also going to watch other smart Weekend Wealth Builders in action as they step into the Money Marketplace and outbid their competitors while insuring themselves against loss. You'll be introduced to both their part-time profit opportunities and their unique moneymaking techniques.

You're going to see my Weekend Wealth Plan in action and learn how you can apply it to your own needs and turn extra time and everyday skills into cash.

SMART MONEY TECHNIQUES FOR GATHERING START-UP AND EXPANSION CAPITAL

One of the greatest things about the Weekend Wealth Plan is that it offers the average person with above-average dreams the opportunity to join the rich and the super-rich. It clearly shows you how to modify the moneymaking techniques used by the big-time business builder and use them to make your spare time more profitable.

You'll soon learn—

How to estimate your Start-Up Capital

How to begin your Weekend Wealth Venture with little or no capital

How the Big Boys use the Power of Leverage for extra profits

How and where to borrow no-risk capital

How to turn unused assets into useful cash

How to find Expansion Capital and multiply it into bigger profits

How to find easy sources for Expansion Capital

How other smart Weekend Wealth Builders use Rented Money profitably

And much more!

QUICKLY DISCOVERING HOW MUCH VENTURE CAPITAL YOU'LL NEED

Venture Capital is the money you will need to start-up your Weekend Wealth Venture and make it profitable. Many smart opportunities can be developed with little or no Venture Capital while others may take $100, $1,000 or more to get going.

Here's how you can decide exactly how much your Weekend Wealth Venture will need to get it on the right track and bring you the extra income you're looking for. Ask yourself these questions:

* What tools, equipment or supplies will I need to begin my Weekend Wealth Venture?
* Can I purchase these items at dealer's cost or at secondhand prices? How much?
* If I'm stocking a product, how much will I have to have on hand when I begin? Can I manage with less by having suppliers drop-ship merchandise for me and thus cut my inventory costs?
* Will suppliers readily offer me a line of credit that allows me to pay for merchandise 30, 60 or 90 days after I receive it? Could I expect to sell the merchandise by then with little cost?
* What overhead should I expect? Will I need an office or can I operate from my home or car? Do I need a business telephone or can I use my home phone until I get going? How can I cut costs on necessary overhead?

How Howard A. Started His Weekend Wealth Venture With Shoestring Venture Capital

Howard A. made a smart decision and planned to start up a weekend tune-up shop. During the week, Howard worked in an auto repair garage in Greeley, Colorado, and had the background to make this a profitable venture. His only problem was coming up with the capital he needed to get his enterprise going.

He decided that he could cut overhead by operating out of his garage and that he wouldn't need a stock of tune-up parts on hand because he could purchase them at wholesale as he needed them from a nearby parts house. His only major expense in starting up would be a diagnostic tune-up machine that cost over $2,000. He knew he didn't have the capital for this.

Then he asked the tune-up machine salesman, who visited his place of work once a month, how he could buy one. The salesman told him that they had just repossessed one from a garage in town that had tried to grow too quickly and now couldn't afford the machine they ordered. Howard could have it if he'd take over the payments on it. He agreed.

Today, Howard operates a chain of three quick tune-up shops in the Greeley area and earns an impressive full-time salary with part-time hours. He did it because he knew how to estimate his Venture Capital needs and search for ways of getting into business with as little cash as possible. Howard is a successful Weekend Wealth Builder who has turned his ideas into a full-time living.

CASHING IN ON THE POWER OF LEVERAGE

A long time ago a smart fellow named Archimedes said,

Give me a place to stand on, and a lever that is long enough, and I can move the world.

Archimedes knew the Power of Leverage. Today this law of physics can be applied profitably to the Money Market-place where power is bought and sold in the form of dollars. Here's how the Power of Leverage can work for you:

* *Rent Money* - You can borrow money from many sources that will be glad to rent it to you and charge you "rent" of 10 to 15 percent interest.
* *Use It Wisely* - You then use my Weekend Wealth Plan to start and operate your own profitable part-time venture.
* *Make More Money* - Your Weekend Wealth Venture then earns you a profit of 25, 50, 100 percent or more on the dollars you've wisely borrowed.

* *Pay Back* - Finally, you return the principal you borrowed, plus the small interest or rent, and keep the substantial difference as the reward for your creative powers as a smart Weekend Wealth Builder.

See how it works? The Power of Leverage has made extra money for many thousands of people who know how to use it. It can do the same for you!

Phyllis S. Turned The Power Of Leverage Into Easy Cash

Let's see how Phyllis S. of Shreveport, Louisiana, used the Power of Leverage profitably.

Phyllis decided to make her part-time profits with an enterprise she would truly enjoy—restoring antiques. After getting a few books on the subject and practicing on second-hand furniture, Phyllis was ready to begin. All she needed was the capital to purchase some antique furniture in rough condition plus the cash for equipment and supplies—a total of about $1,000.

Using techniques that you'll soon learn about for borrowing Rented Money, Phyllis soon had the $1,000 she needed—plus $200 as extra capital. She paid 12 percent "rent" or interest on the money and her payments were just over $32 a month for five years.

Phyllis found that she could make a 300 percent profit by buying rough antique furniture, refinishing it with her equipment and reselling it to anxious buyers. That is, Phyllis was renting money at 12 percent and turning it into a profit of 300 percent. Phyllis was using the Power of Leverage. She's a smart Weekend Wealth Builder.

RENTING VENTURE CAPITAL EVEN IF YOUR CREDIT IS POOR

As you can see, renting your needed capital is the smart way to start your new enterprise. Many Weekend Wealth Builders use the Power of Leverage to get themselves started along the road to part-time profits—even Wealth Builders who have had credit problems in the past.

Here's how they do it:

* *Decide on the best money source* - You'll soon be introduced to a number of sources for Rented Money. Conservative ones need a good credit history and charge a lower rent. Liberal lenders will lend cash to you with few questions, but they charge a higher interest.

* *Show them how you'll spend your money* - Outline your Weekend Wealth Venture plans to them and let them see that your enterprise is worthwhile. Show your lender the potential profits and risk in your venture; then show him how you will minimize risks and maximize profits.

* *Outline repayment* - Your lender will be most interested in how you plan to repay the loan. From profits? From salary at your current job? From selling assets? Let your lender know that your primary concern will be the paying back of Rented Money.

* *Offer Credit History* - If you have good credit built up, let your lender know about it and explain how you've repaid your past loans. If your history is young or not as good, you can stress that his payments will come from your regular job's wages if not from your Weekend Wealth Venture. Paint a positive picture of your desire to repay the loan.

How Floyd E. Rented Venture Capital With Poor Credit

Floyd E., like many people, had a poor credit rating. In fact, that's why he was trying to build up a profitable Weekend Wealth Venture—to clear up old bills and renew his credit.

Floyd's Weekend Wealth Venture was a small magazine for rock collectors in his state. He knew there were over 10,000 active ones and many businessmen who would like to reach them with their message. The problem was that

Floyd decided he'd need about $500 to produce the first issue and he had no capital. Clearly, he needed to find some Rented Money but knew it would be difficult with his credit history.

Floyd outlined his Weekend Wealth Venture on paper showing its purpose, the risk involved, how he could repay the loan from profits, and noted that the salary from his regular job at a travel trailer factory in Elkhart, Indiana, could help make payments if necessary. Even so, the banks turned him down because of his history.

Finally, Floyd went to a printer and talked with him about the enterprise. The printer soon became excited about the venture and offered to let him have it printed on credit for the first issue. The printer even took out an ad in the magazine.

Floyd overcame his credit problem by working with a liberal lender—a supplier—and by showing him on paper how he expected to repay the loan. It worked out very well. Today the *Indiana Rock Hound* is a successful monthly magazine offering Floyd an income of $500 to $800 in extra cash each month—enough to help him clear up his credit and offer a better life to his family.

Floyd E. knows that there are many ways to rent Venture Capital quickly and move toward a profitable Weekend Wealth Venture when you help your lender visualize how he can make a risk-free profit from your ideas.

USING YOUR ASSETS TO BUILD WEEKEND PROFITS

Many smart Weekend Wealth Builders have learned that one of the best ways of getting low-cost Rented Money is to use their assets—things of value—as collateral for the loan. Lenders feel more secure in lending Venture Capital to enterprising people when they insure their loan by offering valuable assets to back it up.

Here's how you can discover your own assets and turn them into an insured loan:

— List your assets: home
                      cars
                      furniture
                      boat
                      trailer
                      tools and equipment
                      insurance policies
                      major appliances

— Estimate their value and, deducting any loans against them to decide how much equity you have in them,

— Offer some or all of these assets as collateral for your loan to insure it and earn the lowest interest rate from the lender.

Cary O. Turned His Assets Into A Profitable Weekend Wealth Venture

To illustrate how the smart Weekend Wealth Builder uses his equity in assets as collateral for Rented Money, let's meet Cary O. of Tallahassee, Florida. He found the perfect enterprise for him: a breeding kennel. He knew there was a great demand for large dogs in his area and wanted to profit from this need by breeding St. Bernards and Labradors. He needed a kennel.

Cary had been paying the mortgage on his home for the past ten years and had built up equity in it. He decided to cash in on this equity and turn it into a Weekend Wealth Venture at home. He did this by going to his bank and securing a small mortgage for part of his equity in the home. With $4,000 in Rented Money, Cary was not only able to build an eight-pen kennel, but he also purchased two show dogs to begin his breeding kennel with.

Cary soon had a profitable kennel that was selling St. Bernard and Lab pups at $200 to $300 each. His cost of daily operation was small and his only expense was the $40 a month in second mortgage payments—and dog food.

You can do the same. You can start your own Weekend Wealth Venture and turn your Time and Skill Building Blocks into extra cash by turning the things you own into collateral for insured loans that smart lenders will be glad to make.

DISCOVERING EXPANSION CAPITAL FOR PYRAMID PROFITS

Once your Weekend Wealth Venture is on its way toward success, you may decide to develop and enlarge your enterprise to bring you even more profits. You'll be ready to use Expansion Capital profitably. Here's how the smart Weekend Wealth Builders do it:

First you decide how much Expansion Capital you're going to need to increase the size—and profits—of your enterprise. Will you need larger or newer equipment? More office or production space? How much? Will you have to hire additional employees?

Then you must estimate how much you can earn in increased profits or Pyramid Profits with your Expansion Capital. Will you double your business? Triple? Increase by 50 percent? Have you checked the market to make sure there is a need and desire for this increased production?

Finally, you must look at it from the lender's standpoint and decide how secure a loan of Rented Money would be to you. Is there a strong potential of low-risk profits? Are there assets that could be used as collateral for the loan?

Here's how one successful Weekend Wealth Builder multiplied his profits with smart Expansion Capital:

Ray H. started a small, part-time venture in his own home, a debt collection business. Ray collected past-due accounts for businessmen in Modesto, California, in exchange for 50 percent of all collected monies. Rather than write them off as bad debts, many smart merchants turned their collections over to Ray. His one-man business prospered.

Then Ray discovered an opportunity to make big money—a large retail chain offered to send all their bad debts to him. Could he handle them on a long-term basis? Yes, but Ray clearly needed some Expansion Capital.

Ray decided that he would need Expansion Capital to rent an office convenient to his major account's office, install more telephones, a copying machine, mailing equipment, and pay a month's salaries for two new employees he'd need. Roughing it out on paper, Ray needed $5,000 in Expansion Capital to turn his Weekend Wealth Venture into a full-time profitable enterprise. Checking the company's records, Ray conservatively estimated he could collect over $20,000 in debts each month for them, half of which would be his.

The bank agreed with Ray's figures and decided to give him the $5,000 loan so he could enlarge his successful venture. He had shown them how he could easily make the payments on the loan from profits. In fact, they were so impressed, the bank asked him to handle some of their collections, too.

Today, Ray's collection agency is the largest in the Modesto area and his salary from the venture is $60,000 a year. Ray's Weekend Wealth Venture quickly grew into a profitable full-time enterprise because he knew how to activate Expansion Capital when he needed it.

So can you!

NINE QUICK SOURCES
FOR VENTURE AND EXPANSION CAPITAL

Whether you're looking for start-up funds or for money to expand and multiply your profits, you can use one or more of these quick cash sources to finance your Weekend Wealth Venture:

* *Commercial Banks* - Your banker is in business to make loans for small enterprises. After you've developed your Weekend Wealth Venture on paper, make an appointment with your banker to secure a small business loan. He may have the money you need waiting for you right now.

* *Credit Unions* - Another excellent source for small loans is your credit union. If you're a member, check into their loan policies to see if you'll qualify. If you're not a member, find out how you can join one.
* *Savings and Loans Associations* - These deal primarily with mortgages on homes, but if you are buying your own home and have equity in it, you may qualify for a second mortgage on your major asset—possibly enough to start or expand your Weekend Wealth Venture.
* *Suppliers* - Many smart Weekend Wealth Builders start with no capital because their suppliers gave them credit on merchandise they purchase. If you're selling a product, this may be your best source of capital. Ask your suppliers.
* *Loan Brokers* - There are probably many loan brokers in your area looking for you. They represent investors who are willing to make loans on small businesses. The brokers find out how much you need, call their clients and "sell" the loan to them. You can find loan brokers in your phone book or in "Money To Loan" classified ads.
* *Finance Companies* - Here's another excellent source of Venture and Expansion Capital. You'll find finance companies in many shopping centers, anxious to loan money for worthwhile purposes. If you can show them that your enterprise is profitable with little risk, they may offer you a substantial loan for your enterprise.
* *Small Business Administration* - Even if you're turned down by many lenders, you can often get the money you want from a loan through the SBA. Check with the SBA in your area to get valuable financial information and see if you qualify for a guaranteed loan. Many thousands of smart Weekend Wealth Builders began with SBA loans.
* *Partners* - Once they've made their fortunes, many small business builders are content to lend their

cash assets to other smart entrepreneurs to begin their enterprises. You can often find a financial partner for your venture by talking with successful businessmen in your area about financing. Try it.

* *Bank Cards* - If you only need a few hundred dollars to start or expand your enterprise, don't overlook bank cards. Many opportunities can be profited from by turning bank cards into quick cash. If you don't have at least two bank cards, sign up for them as soon as possible and use them as a smart source of Weekend Wealth Venture cash.

Don't wait until "tomorrow" to start your profitable Weekend Wealth Venture because you don't have enough capital. Put your enterprise into action today by using one or more of these sources of quick, easy cash to get your enterprise on the road toward profits and satisfaction.

INSURING YOUR LOAN
WITH THE WEEKEND WEALTH PLAN

"Hi ya. I'm Joe Smith and I wanna borrow, oh, about ten thousand for this great business idea I'm working on."

You can already hear the lender's response, can't you? "I'm sorry, Mr. Smith, but we're not currently making small business loans. Thank you anyway."

"Good afternoon, Mr. Lender. My name is Joe Smith and I have a business opportunity that will conservatively return a profit of 26 percent on our investment. The risk has been cut to a minimum. All I need is $4,700 to start this business and operate it for the first two months. Are you interested in making a secured loan?

"Why, yes, Mr. Smith. I think we'd be more than happy to hear about your enterprise. We just might be able to help."

See the difference? Mr. Smith is giving his lender exactly what he wants: facts. Lenders don't deal in emotions and opinions. They only lend cash on facts that add up to a profit for you and for them. Give them what they want and you can discover the key to their vault of funds.

Here's what you need to turn cool lenders into warm friends:

* *Gather your facts.* Lenders won't offer money unless they're satisfied that you know *in advance* exactly what you'll spend it on. Put the facts down on paper: cost of start-up, expected overhead, cost of products or services per unit, estimated income, ways of lowering risk.
* *Slant your facts.* Tell your story with enthusiasm. Describe your Weekend Wealth Venture to your lender in positive terms and show your motivation to make it work and protect his and your investment.
* *Package it up.* Dress up your report neatly so lenders will be impressed with your thoroughness. Present it to them ceremoniously rather than just dropping your report on their desk and leaving. Let them know that you've put a lot of work and thought into your enterprise and you expect them to see its value and make the loan you want.

Duane L. Got Expansion Capital Fast and Easy

Here's how one enterprising Weekend Wealth Builder, Duane L. of Fall River, Massachusetts, raised the capital he needed to raise earthworms, even though his credit was poor.

Duane had all the facts down in rough form. But he knew that the facts didn't tell the whole story. The facts showed that he previously had trouble making some of his payments and had even had a car repossessed. He knew how a lender would feel about those facts. So Duane went back to the creditors that he had problems with and talked. Duane secured a letter from each explaining that, while payments had been slow in the past, Duane had made every effort to make payments as he could and that he was currently in good standing with them.

Duane slanted the facts in his favor.

It worked. By including these letters in his loan folio,

Duane was able to quickly attract a large loan for his enterprise and was soon selling thousands of earthworms each week. Duane's weekend enterprise brought him the cash he needed to clear up old debts and build a new future with my Weekend Wealth Plan.

BUILDING YOUR CREDIT WITH RENTED MONEY

Smart Weekend Wealth Builders know that once they've secured their Venture Capital they can start building the credit they will later need for Expansion Capital. How? By repaying their Venture Capital loan on or ahead of time. Then, when they are ready for more cash, their lender will be ready to help.

Here's how you can insure Rented Money being available when you need it later:

* *Set up a reserve* - Before you spend your first penny of Rented Money, set aside enough to make your loan payment for two or three installments. By doing this, you are insuring that, in case of problems, you'll be able to make your payments on time and keep your good credit intact.

* *Plan repayment* - Talk with your lender about the best way to repay your loan to him. He may allow you to make no payments or make interest-only payments for the first couple of months until you get started.

* *Repay fast* - If profits are good, consider repaying your loan with double payments to lower the total cost of your loan and help build up your credit.

* *Keep your lender informed* - Make sure your Venture Capital lender knows that you are making a good profit with your Weekend Wealth Venture and that you might need an Expansion Capital loan later. He could be your best source for the quick cash you need to grow.

How Scott P. Tailored His Venture Capital
Loan Successfully

Scott P. came up with the right Weekend Wealth Venture for his needs—a small TV repair shop in his garage. He needed $2,600 for equipment to start his enterprise on the road to success.

Just as important, Scott wanted to tailor the terms of his loan to his own needs. He knew that customers wouldn't be paying their bills for at least 30 days and that he would need to cut expenses for the first three months until his venture was on its feet. Here are the terms of the Venture Capital loan that Scott signed:

- $3,000 in cash
- Payments of $200 a month beginning in 90 days
- Right to pay loan off early

As soon as he got the cash, Scott deposited $400—two month's payments—into a second account. He then didn't have to worry about making a payment from profits for a total of five months.

Scott's Weekend Wealth Venture was even more successful than he thought it might be and he was soon making double payments on the balance. The loan was soon paid off. Scott was building his credit.

Then, Scott decided to quit his job as an electronics assembler in a nearby plant and devote full-time to his weekend enterprise. He went to his banker and was quickly approved for a $10,000 loan. Scott had his Expansion Capital in hand and was ready to make the move into a full-time enterprise.

Scott P. knew how to find money that fit his own needs and desires—and how to multiply it into a prosperous business. Scott is a smart Weekend Wealth Builder.

HOW OTHER SUCCESSFUL WEEKEND WEALTH BUILDERS QUICKLY GATHER VENTURE AND EXPANSION CAPITAL

Let's see how two other enterprising people found the capital they needed to start and build a profitable enterprise with the Weekend Wealth Plan:

* Wendell M. decided to start a landscaping service in Austin, Minnesota. He had the tools and the knowledge; all he needed was a pickup truck to haul the

tools and trimmings. Wendell belonged to a credit union through his full-time job so he outlined his needs and opportunity to a loan officer there and found the credit union ready to help. The next afternoon, Wendell had a check for $3,000 to purchase his truck and put his Weekend Wealth Venture on the road to success.

* Jack S. had been operating his venture on the weekends for about six months when he decided to enlarge it with Expansion Capital. Jack was a weekend mechanic who worked on cars in his garage. He soon needed more room. A loan helped Jack rent a larger garage in town. Then, his supplier gave Jack credit to purchase $6,000 worth of needed tools and pay them off over two years. Today Jack operates his auto repair shop five days a week and spends the weekends traveling in his sleek motorhome.

YOU CAN DISCOVER NO-RISK CAPITAL SOURCES TO START AND EXPAND YOUR WEEKEND WEALTH VENTURE

Now you know how ten more smart Weekend Wealth Builders found the funds to turn their ideas into profits with little or no capital.

You've seen them estimate and find Venture Capital to begin their enterprise with Rented Money. You've seen the Power of Leverage in action turning a few dollars into a few thousand dollars.

You have also learned how to build your business once you have perfected it by using the techniques for getting Expansion Capital. Also, you've discovered nine quick sources for Venture and Expansion Capital—sources that can turn your ideas into cash.

You have the tools to increase your value to yourself and to others by profiting from your ideas on how to satisfy the needs and desires of many people. You are a smart Weekend Wealth Builder.

ENERGIZING YOUR WEEKEND WEALTH PLAN

What you now know about raising capital when you need it can be worth thousands of dollars—if you put it into action. Start building your Weekend Wealth right now by doing these things:

1. Quickly decide how much Venture Capital you will need to put your opportunity into action. $20? $100? $1,500? More? What tools, supplies and inventory will you need? What basic costs of overhead will you have?

2. Start right now to turn on the Power of Leverage and increase your Weekend Wealth with Rented Money. Talk with one or more of the money sources in this chapter about your enterprise. Show them how you can easily and profitably pay them back. If you have poor credit, don't let it stand in your way; use the techniques in this chapter to overcome past credit problems.

3. Turn your assets into quick cash either by selling unwanted assets or using them as collateral for a loan. Get off your assets and get moving toward big profits with your Weekend Wealth Venture.

4. Build your credit with Rented Money and move toward the day you can borrow big dollars for expansion of your Weekend Wealth Venture.

5. Review the successes of smart Weekend Wealth Builders in this chapter who have started and built their part-time opportunities into extra income with the techniques of using Rented Money profitably.

Activating Your Weekend Wealth Venture With High Profit Power Tactics

By now you should be a believer in the Weekend Wealth Plan. You've seen over 40 average people turn their time and everyday skills into quick, easy cash. You've watched them start with little or no money and build their income by $100, $300, $500, $1,000 a month and more using Rented Money.

It's time now to activate your Weekend Wealth Plan and join the growing membership of Weekend Wealth Builders. It's time to decide which of the many opportunities you've discovered will be the best one for you—then put it into action and reap your profits.

It's time to make one of the smartest decision you may ever make.

DISCOVERING YOUR BEST WEEKEND WEALTH OPPORTUNITY AND TRANSFORMING IT INTO A WEEKEND WEALTH VENTURE

This may be the most exciting chapter in this book for you. With it you are going to open the wide doors to your future and find the quickest and easiest way to exta income. You're going to review all of the moneymaking techniques you've learned thus far and boil them down into the perfect enterprise for your spare time.

First you'll learn how to gather the best and most profitable opportunities, compare them with your Wealth Building Blocks and personal goals, then make the best and most profitable decision you can. You're going to choose the *right* Weekend Wealth Venture for *you.*

Then you're going to discover how to crystallize your opportunity, how to organize your venture setup, how to start your business on the road towards profits and keep it there.

Excited? I hope so, because you are now on the threshold of a better tomorrow. You are on your way toward realizing your dreams and ambitions of finding extra cash and extra satisfaction in your life with an enterprise that will benefit you and others. You are now ready to start your own unique Weekend Wealth Venture.

Best of luck!

SUMMARIZING THE BEST WEEKEND WEALTH OPPORTUNITIES

You've been exposed to dozens of profitable part-time opportunities—and learned how to develop thousands more. Here's how to quickly narrow them down to one or two of the best ones for you:

* *Review your opportunities*: Look back over the dozens of Weekend Wealth Ventures you've read

about—plus those from other sources—and list the
ones that are most appealing to you.

* *Underscore your favorites*: Mark the ones that you are
  most enthusiastic about. The smart Weekend Wealth
  Builder knows that enthusiasm is his greatest asset
  in building part-time income.
* *Check off your most potential*: Since one of your top
  goals is to build your income, be sure to consider
  opportunities with the highest profit potential.

These are the three steps to cutting down the many
potential weekend enterprises you have around you to the
best ones worthy of your efforts.

How Roger V. Discovered His Top Weekend Wealth Opportunities

Roger V. is an average kind of guy who knew that he
would never get ahead in life if he didn't find an easier way to
gain the things he wanted. His 40-hour-a-week job as a truck
driver for a furntiture store paid his bills, but didn't give him
any extra cash for tomorrow. Roger decided he would invest
a few hours each weekend into building his savings for the
future. Here's how he discovered the best opportunity for
him and put it into action:

First, Roger made a large list of the dozens of Weekend
Wealth Opportunities he could find. He found them in
books, in the telephone book and by observation. All were
potential profit-makers.

Next, Roger marked the ones that he felt he would most
enjoy developing. He knew that the best opportunity for
Weekend Wealth was in a venture that he enjoyed developing. Among his favorite opportunities were:

> Freight broker
> House painter
> Raising pigeons
> Fence builder
> Raising earthworms

Then Roger chose those opportunities that would be the most profitable for him. Of the ones he was most interested in he found that these were also the most profitable:

House painter
Fence builder
Freight broker

Finally, Roger ruled out freight broker because it was speculative. He also ruled out house painter because he would need a great deal of equipment to do it efficiently and profitably—$1,000 worth or more. Roger chose fence builder because he could start within a week and begin making profits his first day with little equipment.

To begin his new venture, Roger talked with lumber companies in the area and told them he would purchase his fencing from them for any job they referred to him. He also put a small ad in an advertising paper in his area. Within the first week he had enough fencing jobs to book up his first month and earn him over $600 in extra cash.

Roger V. knew how to quickly find the most interesting and most profitable Weekend Wealth Venture from the dozens of opportunities available to him.

PROFITABLY MATCHING OPPORTUNITIES WITH YOUR WEALTH BUILDING BLOCKS

Your greatest assets in turning your spare time into quick, easy cash are your Wealth Building Blocks—as you discovered in Chapter 2. They will help make the task of choosing the best opportunity much easier. Here's how to use your Wealth Building Blocks in finding the right part-time opportunity for you:

* *Comparing your Time Blocks* - Check the Time Block you discovered you had in Chapter 2 against those needed for each of the best Weekend Wealth Opportunities. Can this particular opportunity be developed during the time I have available each week?
* *Comparing your Dynamic Skills* - Review your Dynamic Skills of working with people and compare

them against your list of opportunities. Which ventures match your Dynamic Skills best? Do some require public contact more than others? Are your skills high or low in this area?

* *Comparing your Power Skills* - What are your Power Skill Blocks? Do you know how to use special tools or equipment? What opportunities best match these important skills?

* *Comparing Mind Skills* - Ask yourself: What Mind Skill Blocks do I have that can be used in these opportunities? How can I find part-time profits from my Mind Skills?

Steve S. Struck A Gold Mine With His Wealth Building Blocks

Steve S. of Kingston, New York, found his key to Weekend Wealth by matching the many opportunities he had discovered with his greatest assets—his Wealth Building Blocks.

Steve came up with a list of nine Weekend Wealth Opportunities that had both profit potential and sounded interesting. Here's how he narrowed them down with his Wealth Building Blocks:

Steve's Time Block was odd. As a fireman, Steve worked 24 hours, then was off for 48 hours. This schedule cut nearly a third of the opportunities out because they would have to either be on the conventional Saturday-Sunday weekend or at least the same two days each week.

Steve also whittled the list of part-time ventures down by cutting out opportunities that didn't fit his Skill Blocks. Steve was strong in Power Skills and worked well with his hands. He was nearly as strong in Mind Skills and was good at figuring profits and income. His weakest skill was Dynamic Skills—working with people. He worked with many people in his regular job and wanted to work alone on his days off.

By narrowing down his opportunities and eliminating those that didn't specifically match his Wealth Building Blocks, Steve came up with the perfect opportunity for extra profits: making table lamps out of local woods. He could build and market them whenever he had spare time, and he was able to work alone and use his hands to make something that every home needed.

Steve enjoys both his regular job as a fireman and his part-time opportunity of building lamps and turning them into extra cash. Steve knows how to zero in on the opportunities that best utilize his Wealth Building Blocks and also offer him quick profits.

DOUBLE-CHECKING OPPORTUNITIES WITH YOUR GOALS

You can also make sure that the Weekend Wealth Venture you choose is the right one for you by making sure it matches your goals. You've decided that you want a certain amount of cash and satisfaction from your part-time enterprise. Make sure that the opportunity you choose fits these needs. Ask yourself:

* What profit can I realistically expect from this Weekend Wealth Venture? Per hour? Per week? Per month?
* Will expenses increase or decrease as I build my enterprise?
* What is my potential? How much income and profit can I expect once my venture is running smoothly?
* How can I minimize risks from the first day?
* Will this Weekend Wealth Venture satisfy the profit goals I've set for myself? Will it bring me the satisfaction I'm looking for?
* Will this opportunity be a success? How can I insure my success?

DISCOVERING THE BEST WEEKEND WEALTH VENTURE FOR YOU

You're almost there. You've reviewed the most likely opportunities for your profit-making Weekend Wealth Venture. You've compared them with your Wealth Building

Blocks: Time and Skill Blocks. You've even double-checked to make sure that the best candidates will fill your goals and needs for part-time profits.

Now it's time to make your decision and act on it. It's time to put your ideas into action and turn them into the quick, easy cash you're looking for. Here's how smart Weekend Wealth Builders activate their potential and choose the best Weekend Wealth Venture for them. Ask yourself these questions:

* Which opportunity offers the greatest potential for profits with the least risk?
* Which opportunity best utilizes my current Time Blocks and Skill Blocks?
* Which opportunity can be activated the quickest and easiest?
* Which opportunity stands out as the answer to the greatest number of these questions?

How Earl T. Activated The Right Weekend Wealth Venture

Let's talk about Earl T. of Madison, Wisconsin, for a moment. Earl works in the production room of a weekly newspaper in the area. After fourteen years at the same job, Earl was bored by the lack of a challenge. He found little satisfaction in his job and wanted to find a part-time enterprise that would bring him both cash and success.

Earl followed my Weekend Wealth Plan. He quickly learned how to come up with profit opportunities all around him, then narrow them down to a handful, and finally to just three. Here's how Earl chose the best of the three and started it going:

Earl's three opportunities were—

Booklet publisher

Printing broker

Travel agent

Earl began asking himself the questions you just read. Here are his answers:

Greatest profit potential	Printing broker
Greatest satisfaction	Printing broker

Use of Wealth Blocks	Booklet publisher
Activate quickly	Printing broker
Most excited about	Travel agent
Which stands out?	<u>Printing broker</u>

By asking himself a few qualifying questions, Earl narrowed down his choices from three to one—the best one for him. Earl found a special interest in being a printing broker because he could make good money with no investment and it allowed him to utilize his current skills.

Today, Earl represents many printers in the Madison area as he talks with businessmen on his days off and secures printing for them at competitive prices—and collects his commissions. Earl is a successful printing broker who knew how to activate his own Weekend Wealth Venture to find the best profit and satisfaction with his opportunity and skills. Earl is no longer bored with his full-time job. He's put enthusiasm back into his job and is learning new and exciting things about printing. He's reached his personal goals.

DEVELOPING YOUR WEEKEND WEALTH VENTURE CONCEPT

Congratulations!

You've just made one of the best decisions of your future. You've intelligently chosen the best opportunity for you to turn your spare time and skills into extra cash. You've chosen your own Weekend Wealth Venture.

What's next? To develop a profitable concept for your enterprise that will give you a smooth road to success. A Venture Concept is a short statement about your enterprise and how it can serve you by serving others. Here's an example:

Venture Concept: Companion Service
Offering companionship and accompaniment to shut-ins, invalids, and lonely people. Service offers reading to customers, help with housework, shopping and conversation. By the hour or day.

Your Venture Concept helps you define and crystallize your Weekend Wealth Venture by putting your ideas into words. It can also serve to explain to others what product or service you offer. Here's how you can develop your own Venture Concept:

First, write down the title of your Weekend Wealth Venture on a leaf of notebook paper. Examples: "Printing Broker," "Auto Mechanic," "Produce Vendor," or "Debt Collector."

Next, write down as many services as you can that would fall into your category. Under "Hauling Service" you could list: haul trash, recycleable metals, furniture, freight, appliances, small packages, auto parts, and others.

Then, underline the services you would be most interested in offering and scratch out any that you feel would not fit into your concept of this opportunity.

Finally, put your Venture Concept into simple sentences. Explain to yourself and to others exactly what you do and how you do it. Let your customers know what you can do for them and why they will benefit.

How Orville C. Turned An Idea Into A Profitable Venture

Orville C. had little more than an idea when he first decided to put profits in his weekends with a part-time business opportunity. Then he learned about crystallizing his plans with a Venture Concept.

Orville worked in an accountant's office in Portland, Oregon, all week. After 40 hours of reconciliations and posting debits and credits, Orville was ready for something that didn't take a lot of Mind Skills. He decided to capitalize on his hobby, raising house plants.

To develop his Venture Concept, Orville first wrote down his venture idea, "Raising House Plants," then made a list of all the ways he could profit from this venture. He wrote:

Raise only a few varieties to sell to retailers

Raise a wide variety for sale to the public

- Sell from a small stand in a shopping mall

- Sell from door-to-door
- Sell by mail order

Include written instruction on care with each plant

Rent large plants to offices; include care as part of service

Then Orville underscored the ideas that most appealed to him: selling plants through retailers and including instructions on their care. This was his Venture Concept. Orville decided to become a wholesaler of African Violets and he built a small nursery onto the side of his garage.

By developing his Venture Concept, Orville was able to discover the best Weekend Wealth Venture for him and turn it into a profitable and enjoyable part-time opportunity. Today, Orville spends a couple of relaxing hours each evening and four hours on Saturday taking care of his profitable venture. He enjoys his new business—and the $500 to $600 a month in extra income it offers him.

Orville C. is a satisfied Weekend Wealth Builder.

SETTING UP YOUR WEEKEND WEALTH VENTURE FOR QUICK AND EASY PROFITS

You're now ready to turn your Venture Concept into a profitable part-time business. Here are six easy steps to follow in activating your Weekend Wealth Venture now and turning your ideas into cash this weekend:

* *Choose your name* - Once you've defined your Venture Concept, you should choose a name for your business. It can include your own name (Pete's Tune-Up Service), the name of your town (Montrose Auction Company), or a general business name (Ace Pet Company).

* *Open your bank account* - With a small amount of cash, you can open your business checking account at a nearby bank and purchase printed checks.

* *Start your credit* - While you're at the bank, introduce yourself to a bank officer and outline your business idea. You'll find a valuable friend. He may offer ideas

on how to make your venture more profitable and offer to help you with business loans. You can also establish credit by taking out a small loan and repaying it in a short time.

* *Set up your books* - You'll want to keep track of every dollar you make and spend. The Internal Revenue Service, of course, will be interested—but you should be moreso. A good set of books will tell you how and where your income and expenses flow. You can use these facts to make your venture more profitable. You'll learn how to set up a profitable record-keeping system in Chapter 11.

* *Gather equipment* - Make a list of the tools and equipment you'll need in your part-time business and begin gathering them. If you offer a service, you'll still want a phone, a file and possibly a typewriter. Start with used equipment if possible.

* *Build your inventory* - If you sell a product, start gathering some of your inventory so you'll have products to sell to your first customers. If you sell a service, build your inventory of ideas on how to best service them efficiently and profitably.

Once you've followed these six steps to venture set-up you'll be ready to turn your first customers into profits and move your Weekend Wealth Venture toward success.

ACTIVATING YOUR WEEKEND WEALTH VENTURE PROFITABLY

Here comes your first customer!

You've chosen the best part-time opportunity for your needs, you've developed it into a smart venture, and you've set up your venture in preparation for your first transaction.

Here's how you can turn your first customer into your first profit dollar:

* Find your customer's need
* Fill your customer's need

* Show him that value is greater than cost
* Trade your product or service for cash

It's as simple as that. To illustrate this four-step system for profiting from each customer, let's see—

How Sid and Barbara K. Activated Their Venture And Turned Their First Customer Into A Quick And Easy Profit

Sid and Barbara K. of Vancouver, British Columbia, worked in the same office—the head office of a major Canadian insurance company. They wanted a business opportunity that they could operate part-time and take advantage of the many daily contacts they had with fellow employees. They also enjoyed traveling.

The K's decided to start a part-time travel agency. By taking evening classes they soon had the background for the Weekend Wealth Venture they wanted to start: offering vacation packages to employees where they worked. Once they set up their firm, New World Travel, they spread the word via a small ad in their company newsletter and prepared themselves for their first customer.

He soon arrived. George N. asked them what type of vacation packages they offered. This is how they handled his request for information:

Find Need	What would you enjoy doing during your vacation? How much time do you have off? When? How much would you like to spend on your vacation? Are there any special places you'd like to see?
Fill Need	Here's a popular three-island tour of Hawaii that fits your needs and is just $425.
Value Greater Than Cost	Imagine spending seven warm days and eight balmy eve-

| | nings in the most beautiful of all tropical islands. You'll come back refreshed and relaxed—ready to face your job with renewed vitality. You can use your bank card to spread the payments out and pay just a few dollars each month. |
| Trade For Cash | You can make your check out to New World Travel and we'll take care of everything. |

By using this simple four-step system for turning customers into profits, Sid and Barbara K. turned their spare time into an extra income that averaged $650 a month—summer and winter. The K.'s are smart Weekend Wealth Builders who know how to find their customers' needs, fill them, then show them how they will benefit from the right decision.

You can adapt their system to any product or service you build with the Weekend Wealth Plan. Try it.

TURNING YOURSELF ON FOR SUCCESS

Motivation is one of the greatest tools available to the person who wants to move quickly through the crowd. The Power of Motivation will open doors for you by helping you persuade others of the value of your ideas. The Power of Self-Motivation is just as important because it will help you see the value in your own ideas—and help you move toward succeeding with them.

To turn others on to the benefits of your Weekend Wealth Venture *you* must first be turned on to them. Here's how the smart Weekend Wealth Builders use the Power of

Self-Motivation to build positive futures for both themselves and their customers:

* *Believe in the need* - There is a need for the product or service you sell. It may be a great need like the need for food or shelter—or it may be a smaller need for prestige, comfort or self-image. All need to be filled. Recognize the need that others have for what you have to offer.

* *Believe in the value* - Your enterprise also has value to others. By filling a need for them it is enriching their lives. It is improving their situation. If they are willing to trade the money they have for something you can offer them, that product or service has value to others. Recognize that value and remember that as you profit others will profit.

* *Work for goal satisfaction* - If you have a part-time enterprise, your first goal is to profit and your other goal is to help others reach their own goals with your product or service. Your customer's main goal is to benefit from your venture and his second goal, realized or not, is to offer you enough money to make you part with something that will satisfy his goal. In other words, the customer is interested in your making a profit. If you make your aim in business the satisfaction of goals, Weekend Wealth will come to you.

How Kent P. Turned Himself On To Succeed With His Weekend Wealth Venture

Kent P. of Fairbanks, Alaska, decided to start a small appliance repair business to turn his weekends into wealth.

The problem was, Kent couldn't see much value to the idea of repairing small appliances. He just didn't think it was something that was very necessary. He couldn't motivate himself to start his business.

Then he discovered the Power of Self-Motivation and

sat down to analyze his Weekend Wealth Venture. Here's what Kent wrote down on a slip of paper:

"Need - *Most people don't really need appliances repaired. Old ones break and they just throw them away and buy new ones. Of course, there are many people who really can't afford to buy new ones and they may need to have someone who knows how the appliances work to fix them at a reasonable cost. And many people would rather repair an older appliance that was built solidly than buy some of the new appliances that aren't made as well. Yes, I guess there is a need for a small appliance repair service."*

"Value - *But who would want to trade their hard-earned dollars for repairs that many people could do themselves if they had the tools and a few books on the subject? Sure, most people are afraid to work with electricity and would rather have someone experienced with it to fix their appliances. And for many people, fixing an old appliance is a better buy than purchasing a new one. Well, actually, there is a value to my service–savings and peace of mind.*

"Goal satisfaction - *My goal is to make a profit by offering my time and skills to others. My customer's goal is to have his small appliances repaired and put back into good working condition for a reasonable cost. If I can help the customer meet his goals, I will be meeting mine. That's the way I want it to be: I offer a needed and valuable service to others in exchange for the money I need to satisfy my own goals. I can see that as long as I help my customers reach their goals I will reach mine. I'm motivated now to start my potentially-successful Weekend Wealth Venture.*

And Kent did. Today he earns more than ten dollars an hour repairing small appliances because he keeps his customers' goals utmost in his mind. Kent is a succcessful Weekend Wealth Builder.

HOW OTHER AVERAGE PEOPLE HAVE CHOSEN AND ACTIVATED THEIR WEEKEND WEALTH VENTURES

See how easy it is to reach your own goals in life? Thousands of everyday people from all walks of life and every part of the country have turned their spare time—evenings, weekends, days off—into extra cash.

Before we end this chapter, I'd like you to meet a few more successful Weekend Wealth Builders:

* Henry B. had a problem. He found two ventures that he wanted to develop as part-time moneymakers. He wanted to be a sign maker *and* a part time handyman. The solution? Henry decided to do both. Since he only needed a few dollars for additional tools and supplies, Henry could start them both with little cash. Today he offers both a fix-it service and sign painting during his spare hours. Between the two, Henry earned an extra $6,300 last year.

* Willie J. had the perfect Weekend Wealth Venture for his Time and Skill Blocks: Willie worked as a salesman, on commission, at a used car lot on Saturdays. Willie enjoyed both cars and people. To make the greatest profit, Willie decided to develop his Venture Concept to fit both his own philosophy and other people's needs. His concept was: "Help each customer find the right car for himself and help him make the decision to buy it. Follow the 'Golden Rule.'" Willie's concept gave him the attitude that helped him earn as much as $500 in a single weekend.

YOU CAN DISCOVER YOUR WEEKEND WEALTH VENTURE AND TURN IT INTO CASH

You can find the satisfaction and profit you're searching for with my Weekend Wealth Plan. You can see the successes of more than one hundred successful Weekend Wealth Builders unfold on these pages and give you the knowledge and confidence to follow the well-traveled path to extra cash.

You've learned how to discover the best Weekend Wealth Venture for you and transform it into a money-making opportunity. You've reviewed dozens of profit opportunities and chosen the best one. You've matched these ventures with your own Wealth Building Blocks. You've made sure that your chosen venture will take you to your own goals. And you've made the decision to activate the Weekend Wealth Venture that offers you and others the greatest benefits.

You've also learned how to develop your own Venture Concept to crystallize your opportunities for profit; you've chosen the name of your business and started it on the road to success. Finally, you've turned yourself on to the many opportunities you have with your venture with the Power of Self-Motivation.

You've discovered the high profit power tactics that can change your ideas into cool cash. You've discovered the powerful Weekend Wealth Plan.

ENERGIZING YOUR WEEKEND WEALTH PLAN

You may want to mark this day on you calendar and look back on it as the turning point in your life. This is the day you are going to activate your Weekend Wealth Venture and start making extra money with your ideas. Here's how:

1. Summarize the best Weekend Wealth Opportunities you've discovered thus far. Which have the most potential for profits? Which offer you the most satisfaction? How would you rate each on a scale of one to ten?

2. Match your opportunities with your Wealth Building Blocks. Which of these ventures best fits the time and skills that you have available? Compare with your Dynamic, Power and Mind Skills.

3. Review your own goals to make sure that the top two or three opportunities you're considering are ones that will bring you the success, wealth and happiness you're searching for.

4. Once you've decided on *the* Weekend Wealth Venture for you, develop your Venture Concept to help you define your opportunity to yourself and its benefits to your customers. This is a very important step.

5. Set up your Weekend Wealth Venture this week. Make a list right now of the things you can do to put your venture on the road to success: choose your business name, open your bank account, start building your credit, set up your record system, gather needed equipment and build your inventory of products and services.

6. Finally, turn yourself on to the success you can find with the Power of Self-Motivation. Visualize how you can help yourself and others with your profitable Weekend Wealth Venture.

How Smart Weekend Wealth Builders Guarantee Their Fortunes

How would you like to minimize the risks that others face in starting a new business?

You can—with my Weekend Wealth Plan. You can follow the lead of hundreds of other people who have learned to cut losses to nearly zero percent while they increase profits to one-hundred percent of their potential.

You can turn other people's mistakes into your own profits. You can discover Risk-Free Wealth. You can take out a Success Insurance Policy. You can actually *guarantee* yourself profits from your Weekend Wealth Venture by following the simple steps in this chapter.

And, again, you'll be guided every step of the way—you'll see each principal and rule illustrated—by many successful Weekend Wealth Builders who know how to minimize risks and maximize profits with my Weekend Plan.

Let's move into action!

HOW TO ANALYZE AND MINIMIZE RISKS IN YOUR WEEKEND WEALTH PLAN

Smart Weekend Wealth Builders know how to keep thousands of extra dollars that others lose to the learning process of building a profitable business. The Weekend Wealth Builder has learned how to test his opportunity on paper *before* he invests his time and skills to insure that every aspect of his venture is workable and profitable.

You'll soon learn how they Pre-Test Profitability.

You'll also see the four dynamic steps to Risk-Free Wealth in action—taking the hazards out of operating any business opportunity:

* *Success Insurance* - You'll write yourself a Success Insurance Policy and trim away risks
* *Capital Security* - You'll learn how to minimize losses by making only reversible capital purchases
* *Dynamic Planning* - You'll draw your own map to success and follow the clearly marked path
* *Neutralize Failure* - Mistakes are inevitable. You'll learn a unique method of profiting from every one.

And, of course, you'll see each point illustrated by successful Weekend Wealth Builders who will give you new business ideas and profitable methods.

TESTING YOUR VENTURE FOR MARKET PRACTICALITY

To be successful, your Weekend Wealth Venture must fill a need or desire for others. This is true whether you're offering a dog-grooming service or candy apples. So to make sure that you are building a potentially successful venture, test your opportunity before you invest your first dollar. Identify your potential customers and ask them questions like:

* Would you use my product or service?
* How much would you be willing to pay for it?
* Are you using a similar product or service?
* How much do you pay for it?
* What improvements would you like to see made in this product or service?
* How often would you use this product or service?

These Profit Probes will help you define your own customers' needs and desires—plus help you discover how much they would be willing to pay for what you have to offer.

How Edna J. Turned Profit Probes Into A Successful Weekend Wealth Venture

Edna J. offers a good example of how to pre-test your opportunity and earn extra cash the easy way. Edna was a secretary in an oil company's Houston, Texas, office when she discovered that she could increase her income in just a few hours each week with a Weekend Wealth Venture.

Edna decided that she would like to offer a Publicity Service for small businessmen in Houston. To make sure that this was an opportunity that was practical, Edna spent two lunch hours on the phone talking with potential customers about her venture. She asked them:

Would you like to increase profits by improving your image to your customers and potential customers?

Would you be willing to invest a few dollars in image building? How many?

What results would you like to see from such a campaign?

Would you like to offer your customers and friends a newsletter about developments in your common fields?

*Would you like to develop product literature about
your business?*
*Would you prefer to hire a Publicity Service by the
hour as needed or on a retainer basis?*

Edna's Profit Probes were successful. Not only was she
able to discover the dimensions of the need for her Publicity
Service, she also lined up her first customers for the service
and began profiting from her venture that next weekend.

Edna J. of Houston, Texas, now operates a full-time
public relations firm for small businesses throughout Texas
and surrounding states because she tested her venture for
market practicality *before* investing her valuable time and
money. She's a smart—and wealthy—Weekend Wealth
Builder.

ANALYZING SELF-PRACTICALITY

Of course, your Weekend Wealth Venture must also fit
your needs and desires as well as those of your potential
customers. Here's a quick review of how you can make sure
that your venture will bring you the things you desire. Ask
yourself:

* Will this Weekend Wealth Venture fulfill my profit
  goals?
* Will I enjoy operating this venture or will it be just
  another job?
* Can I expand the venture to allow me to hire others
  for menial tasks and give me more spare time while
  still making a profit?
* Will I learn profitable business concepts by operating this business?
* Is this the best Weekend Wealth Venture for me?

Let's see—

How One Weekend Wealth Builder Tested
His Venture's Self-Practicality

Ron N. discovered what he felt was a good Weekend
Wealth Venture. To make sure, Ron began asking himself

questions similar to the ones you have just read. Here's the result:

Ron decided he wanted to open a rock shop in a nearby shopping center on weekends. He enjoyed working with rocks and lapidary equipment and felt that there were enough rock hounds in Flagstaff, Arizona, to keep him busy selling supplies two days a week.

By asking himself questions about whether this Weekend Wealth Venture fit his own needs and desires, Ron discovered a few things. He discovered that he could probably turn a small profit while enjoying his venture, but that expenses would be high and it might take him a year or two to build it up to a highly profitable venture. He had to cut expenses.

His major expense, of course, was rent for a store that would be closed five days a week. He considered setting up the rock shop in his own home, but he lived too far out of town to ask customers to travel to him. It would take too much expensive advertising to draw them out that far.

Studying the practicality of his venture, Ron finally hit upon the answer: he would share a store with a related business. He soon found a major shopping center that had a large hobby shop in it. He approached the owner and offered to set up his weekend rock shop in the store and pay a percentage of his income as rent for the space. The hobby shop owner saw the value of Ron's offer and accepted it.

During the week, Ron N. installs cabinets in new homes; but on the weekend, he is a successful rock shop operator because he joined forces with another smart entrepreneur and built his Weekend Wealth with Self-Practicality.

QUICKLY TESTING VENTURE PROFITABILITY

You can insure your success with your Weekend Wealth Venture before you earn your first dollar by testing the profitability of your enterprise on paper. Once you've chosen your opportunity and developed your Venture Concept, ask yourself these questions:

* Who will use my product or service?
* How often will they use it?
* How much will they pay for it?
* What can I expect as an income?
* How much will this income fluctuate?
* Will it change seasonally? How much?
* What can I do to increase this income during slower times?
* What simple modifications could I make in my enterprise to develop a new and more profitable market for my venture?

By testing venture profitability on paper, before you invest your own time and money in your enterprise, you are minimizing the risk of loss and maximizing your profits. You are working like a smart Weekend Wealth Builder.

To cut risks even more, you can increase profitability by asking yourself these questions about expenses in your Weekend Wealth Venture:

* How can I cut overhead costs easily while still holding up income?
* What's the best and most profitable location for my enterprise? Home or store front? Garage or corner lot? Front yard or shopping center parking lot?
* What one-time expenses will I have in setting up my enterprise and how can I minimize them?
* What ongoing expenses should I expect? Should I start my venture offering full services or should I build up to it after the enterprise is off the ground?
* Will I have production costs? If so, how can I minimize them until my venture has proven itself?

How Dennis G. Saved Four Thousand Dollars By Testing Venture Profitability First

Dennis G. was a do-it-yourselfer who saw a real need for home delivery of cement in his hometown of Whittier, California.

Dennis' plan was to purchase a small cement mixer and secondhand pickup truck to deliver cement to customers on weekends. He discovered that a heavy duty mixer would cost him about $2,000 and that a pickup truck would cost another $2,000 plus his old car. But Dennis didn't have $4,000 in cash to invest in a part-time enterprise.

After reviewing his venture on paper for profitability, Dennis decided that the market for his service was there if he could reach it economically. He had to find a low capital method of starting his Weekend Wealth Venture. Then a friend suggested that Dennis rent a mixer from a rental yard in nearby Norwalk and pull it with a bumper hitch on his old car. He could always use the trunk to haul extra tools.

That weekend, Dennis was hauling his first load of cement to help a customer pour a patio—at a healthy profit. Dennis had discovered a low-cost way to start his enterprise quickly by reviewing Venture Profitability and finding alternative methods of securing needed equipment. Dennis now earns between $100 and $200 each and every Saturday and he's usually booked up weeks in advance. Dennis saved thousands of dollars in profits by using the Weekend Wealth Plan.

WRITING YOUR OWN SUCCESS INSURANCE POLICY

How would you like to insure yourself for success in your Weekend Wealth Venture?

You can by underwriting your own Success Insurance Policy—and naming yourself as beneficiary. Here's how the smart Weekend Wealth Builders insure their own success:

* *Ask yourself "What if...?"* - Here's one of the greatest keys to being prepared for any situation. Once you've established your business idea in your mind and know how you will operate it, ask yourself "What if my customers drop off?"; "What if I can't find enough raw materials?"; "What if my costs triple in a short time?"; "What if my venture doesn't work?"
* *Prepare for obstacles* - Then take steps to neutralize possible problems before they occur. Prepare a con-

tingency plan and decide what you'd do if you did lose many of your customers, if raw materials became scarce, or if your venture didn't work. Be prepared.

* *Pay the premium* - The cost of insurance is always less than its value. Your Success Insurance Policy will cost you only a few dollars or a few hours in research and planning. It may be the cost of developing alternate suppliers or related products and services or building an alternate Weekend Wealth Plan. The cost is small compared to the benefits of venture success.

* *Minimize risks* - You can improve the benefits of your Success Insurance Policy while reducing the premium costs by discovering ways of cutting the risk of loss: renting equipment before you buy, testing the market slowly, keeping expenses down until income justifies increases, using other people's money.

How Phil B. Insured Success In His Weekend Wealth Venture

Phil B. of Jacksonville, Florida, wrote his own valuable Success Insurance Policy when he set up his Weekend Wealth Venture—a flea market. Here's how he did it:

Phil outlined his Venture Concept as offering "a convenient and practical location for buyers and sellers of secondhand, craft and miscellaneous items to get together." To write his own Success Insurance Policy, Phil asked himself "What if ... few sellers rented tables from me?"; "What if ... I don't draw enough buyers in to the flea mart to make it profitable?" and "What if ... weather ruins the flea mart?"

Phil set about to face these potential obstacles to success *before* they happened. First, Phil developed a promotional campaign to let everyone in the area know about his flea mart. Even smarter, Phil offered one of the smaller Jacksonville radio stations ten cents of every quarter he collected as admission to the flea mart as payment for advertising. Phil also offered the owner of a vacant warehouse five cents from every quarter as rent for an indoor flea mart.

Smart thinking. Phil had now answered his potential problems—too few sellers, too few buyers and inclement weather. His two major costs, advertising and space rent, were now decided by the number of people attending the flea mart rather than by paying a flat fee or rent.

The flea mart was a huge success. Twenty-three tables were rented at ten dollars each and more than 1,600 people paid 25 cents each to come in and browse through the bargains. After paying agreed costs to the radio station and warehouse owner, Phil was left with a handsome profit of $355 for a six-hour flea mart. Best of all, Phil used none of his own capital and had even written his own Success Insurance Policy to make sure everything worked out profitably.

GENERATING 100 PERCENT CAPITAL SECURITY

Here's another way you can minimize the normal risks that other enterprising Weekend Wealth Builders must face. Here's how to build your venture with reversible capital purchases and further insure yourself for success. All you have to do is follow these four steps to Capital Security when building your Weekend Wealth Venture:

* *Never buy "Blue Sky"* - Blue Sky is a term for goodwill or an intangible asset built by a good name. If you purchase a business or major equipment from another, only pay the price of the equipment or assets and not for the "name" that the business has built up. Blue Sky is difficult to resell.

* *Buy reuseable assets* - Anything you buy for your venture should either be turned into a salable product or service—or be used many times to manufacture this product or service. Find marketable uses for all waste.

* *Buy right* - The rule of the smart Weekend Wealth Builder is "Never buy anything that you can't turn around and sell for at least the same price." If you purchase a piece of needed equipment, never buy it for more than an easy resale price. This often means

buying drastically reduced new equipment or well-priced used equipment in good repair.

* *Keep your assets liquid* - This means you should make sure that you can quickly turn the things you buy for your business into cash if needed. Make sure you have a profitable market for the things you buy. You'll be insuring your own success.

How Don L. Developed His Risk-Free Weekend Wealth Venture

I'd like to illustrate this important system for building your venture with 100 percent Capital Security with the story of Don L. of Sitka, Alaska.

Don's Weekend Wealth Venture was to export Eskimo handicrafts to the other 49 states. Beyond the crafts he would need, Don decided that he would need some office equipment and supplies. He had a total of $400 to invest in his part time enterprise.

To insure his success, Don purchased a used typewriter and file cabinet from a real estate office that was closing its doors. The equipment was only a year old, but Don was able to buy it for about twenty cents on the dollar. He bought it for about half of what he could resell the individual pieces for. He was not buying the Blue Sky of a new machine and file cabinet and he was making sure that the assets were reuseable. Finally, Don knew of two other small business operators who would quickly buy the equipment from him for a profit. His assets were liquid and easy to turn into cash if he needed it for a big expansion.

Don is a smart Weekend Wealth Builder who knows how to insure his venture's success with 100 percent Capital Security.

MINIMIZING RISKS WITH DYNAMIC PLANNING

As you've learned throughout this book, the greatest path to Weekend Wealth is the one you know the best. You've chosen a clearly-marked path laid out by other smart entrepreneurs. You've decided on your own destination based on your needs and desires. You've seen yourself in your imagination reaching each checkpoint along the road to success. You've written your own future and moved toward enjoying it.

The importance of Dynamic Planning—choosing your own destination and marking out the road ahead of you—can't be stressed too much. It is one of the golden keys to part-time profits. Let's double-check to make sure you have your goals and plan clearly in mind before you go any farther. By doing so, you'll be minimizing risks and increasing the face value of your Success Insurance Policy. Ask yourself:

* What Weekend Wealth Venture have I chosen?
* What is my Venture Concept?
* What goal do I want to reach with my venture? When?
* What is the first thing I must do to start on my road to success?
* What other things must I do to reach my chosen goal?
* How can I minimize risks and maximize my potential profits?
* Who are my customers and how can I best reach them?
* What profits can I realistically expect from this Weekend Wealth Venture?
* How can I decrease risks and increase profits with Market Practicality? Self-Practicality?
* Have I put my ideas for this Weekend Wealth Venture down on paper? Do I devote a few minutes each day to reviewing these ideas and discovering better ways to success?
* Have I prepared myself for the fulfilling profits and personal satisfaction I'll earn with my successful Weekend Wealth Venture?

If you can answer these questions positively, congratulations, you're definitely on your way to Weekend Wealth.

HOW TO QUICKLY NEUTRALIZE FAILURE

You can completely remove "failure" from your vocabulary and exchange it for the sweet sound of "success" with the Weekend Wealth Plan. Here's how:

Failure is nothing more than an attitude. You fail at a task because you *think* you fail. If your venture faces a setback, you can face the problem with a solution and bring yourself closer to success by capitalizing on the lessons you learn. You can find the silver lining in every cloud if you'll turn so-called failures into profitable situations by doing these things:

* *Always work toward success* - Assume that each task you perform will be successful. See setbacks as opportunities to build greater successes. Never let little problems stand in your way.

* *Turn problems into solutions* - Once you face an obstacle, stop to analyze it for the most profitable solution. You can often discover that overcoming a problem can be more profitable to you than having a smooth road. Look at problems not as failures, but as opportunities for success.

* *Learn from every situation* - Everything you do on your road to success has a lesson for you—and each lesson you learn will help you reach your goal.

How Dale H. Overcame Failure

Dale H. of Waterbury, Connecticut, was afraid to fail—until he learned that the opportunity for failure is actually an opportunity to succeed.

Dale's Weekend Wealth Venture was not a business, but a career. He wanted to be a disc jockey on a local radio station on the weekends. The problem was that Dale was afraid to talk to radio program directors in his area about being hired as a deejay. He took courses at broadcast school, but he was afraid of failure when applying for jobs.

Finally, Dale faced facts and told himself that the opportunity for failure that he was afraid of was also an opportunity for success. He knew he couldn't succeed until he tried and that a "no" couldn't be taken as a personal failure. Dale realized that when someone told him "no" they were saying "no, I can't use your idea," not "no, I don't accept you."

At each interview for a job, Dale learned what the program directors wanted—and what they didn't want. He learned from both the positive and negative comments they offered. Results? Dale learned that new disc jockeys with a positive attitude were much in demand as weekend employees at most radio stations and that each turn-down was actually an opportunity to succeed with the lessons learned. Dale now earns a handsome salary for the six hours each Saturday evening he spends as a weekend disc jockey on a Waterbury radio station.

Dale has found that stepping over obstacles can take you higher on your road to success as a Weekend Wealth Builder.

YOUR CHECKLIST FOR RISK-FREE PROFITS

Here are a few more valuable points you can check to make sure that your Weekend Wealth Venture will bring you the success you deserve:

Have I carefully investigated this opportunity?

Do I know what type of profit to expect?

Have I discovered who my potential customers are?

Do I know how to reach these customers quickly and easily?

Do I know what the potential problems are in this venture?

Am I prepared to turn potential problems into opportunities for success?

Does this venture have a good future?

How can I quickly cut expenses if necessary?

What extra profits can I find to help insure my success with this venture?

How can I do better than my competition?

Will this venture bring me to my goals?

YOU CAN PROFITABLY TEST YOUR WEEKEND WEALTH VENTURE AND MINIMIZE RISKS

You've seen how smart Weekend Wealth Builders actually *guarantee* their fortunes by testing their ventures on paper and facing each problem before it happens.

You can use the steps to success in this chapter to cut your own opportunity for potential losses to nearly zero percent by Pre-Testing Profitability.

You can also write your own Success Insurance Policy and use the principles of Capital Security and Dynamic Planning to neutralize failure and turn every potential problem into a profitable success.

You can build your part-time income with little risk as you learn and use my Weekend Wealth Plan.

ENERGIZING YOUR WEEKEND WEALTH PLAN

Here's how to save thousands of dollars in starting and operating your Weekend Wealth Venture by testing your opportunity on paper and minimizing risks before they occur:

1. Test your venture for Market Practicality and Self-Practicality to make sure that it will meet both the needs of your customers and you. Use the Profit Probes offered in this chapter.
2. Test Venture Profitability by answering the questions in this chapter about income, expenses and potential profits available with your enterprise. They can save you countless hours and many dollars.
3. Write your own Success Insurance Policy by asking yourself "What if...?" and planning for potential obstacles to your success. Develop your own contingency plan.

4. Minimize losses with 100 percent Capital Security. Purchase capital assets and supplies wisely and make sure they can easily be resold.
5. Neutralize potential failures in your enterprise by building an attitude of success that can turn problems into solutions quickly. Profit from mistakes.

Using The Power
Of Dynamic Motivation
To Multiply Your Profits

It's time to turn what you've learned from other smart Weekend Wealth Builders into part-time profits for yourself.

So far, your profits have been on paper. You've analyzed your own needs, compared them with the many Weekend Wealth opportunities available, chosen the right one for you, learned how to gather starting capital, and cut risks to a minimum as you maximized profits. Now you can put this valuable knowledge into action as you start up and market your Weekend Wealth Venture for immediate profits.

Again, you're learning from the combined experience of hundreds of people much like yourself who have the ambition and desire to turn extra hours into spendable cash. You're joining the *Golden Circle of Wealth*–the Weekend Wealth Builders who have put their ideas into action and profited from them.

Best of luck.

TURNING ON YOUR WEEKEND WEALTH VENTURE PROFITABLY

You've come a long way since you first opened this book. I think you're ready to learn and use the Weekend Wealth-Building Techniques in this chapter to exchange your spare time for big profits. Here's what you'll learn:

* How to develop your product or service to meet the widest and most profitable market
* How to discover your venture's cost per unit/hour and estimate profits quickly
* How to add thousands of dollars in extra profits to your venture with Management Magic
* How to make your customers come to you
* How to profitably go to your customers and sell them your product or service
* How to use Dynamic Motivation to get professional sales people to work for you
* How to use other profitable systems for distributing your product or service to those who will quickly buy from you

Excited? I hope so. I hope you can see the value of these advanced Weekend Wealth-Building Techniques that have made millions of dollars in total profits for other entrepreneurs.

PROFITABLY DEVELOPING YOUR WEEKEND WEALTH VENTURE PRODUCT

Maybe you've decided to build your spare time income with a product that is valuable to others. If so, in the next few pages you'll learn how to develop your product for the right market and turn it into cash.

First, ask yourself: What would this Venture Product be used for? Is it used in the home? Garage? Car? Yard? At work? In an office? At the beach? What need will it fill—and for whom?

Next, decide how this Venture Product can best fill its intended need. What function does it have? What must it do for its owner in order to be valuable to him or her? See this product in use.

Then, consider other possible uses for your Venture Product. Who else might benefit from your product? How would they use it? What unique uses and applications can you find for this product?

Finally, ask yourself: What is this Venture Product worth to others? Will it help them enjoy life more? Make more money? How much will they profit from its use? How much cash would they exchange for it?

How George P. Turned A Simple Product Into A Healthy Profit

George P. of Flint, Michigan, had the right idea. He chose picture frames as his Weekend Wealth Venture Product and took a few minutes to consider how he was going to profitably develop his product with the four steps you just learned.

George asked himself what the product was normally used for and answered that it was both practical and decorative. It would be used in the home, in an office and wherever paintings were hung.

George decided that to best fill its intended need it should be sturdy and ornamental. It should be made of high-quality woods, have a lasting finish and a decorative design that would complement, but not detract from, the painting it framed.

Then George considered other uses for his picture frames. He came up with these:

- Mirror frames
- Decorative door and window moldings

- Photo frames
- Table top edging

Finally, George considered the value of his picture-framing service. Since a high-quality frame often added value to the picture it held, George decided the frame should be worth at least 25 percent of the value of the picture. With this formula, George estimated the value of his frames at from $15 to $100 each depending on size and design. These figures were competitive with other picture framers in his area—and offered him a markup of 400 percent over costs.

George spends six hours on Saturdays filling orders for picture frames and makes as much as $200 a weekend because he learned how to profitably develop his Venture Product into the cash he wanted. George is a very successful Weekend Wealth Builder.

GENERATING EXTRA CASH WITH YOUR VENTURE SERVICE

You can use the same easy system for developing your Venture Service and building it into a spare time enterprise. Simply ask yourself:

* Who would use my Venture Service?
* How would they use it?
* Where would they use it?
* What must this service do for my customers to be of value to them?
* How can it best fulfill this need?
* What other uses can this service be put to? By whom?
* What is this service worth to others? How much will they profit from its use? How much cash would they be willing to exchange for its benefits?

To illustrate how you can develop new and profitable ideas for your Weekend Wealth Venture, let's meet Kenny R. of Hagerstown, Maryland.

Kenny discovered the right Weekend Wealth Venture for his Time and Skill Blocks—operating a chauffeur service. His Venture Concept was to "offer scheduled and nonscheduled transportation to and from homes, work, entertainment spots and transportation depots in Hagerstown and Frederick, Maryland."

Great idea. But Kenny wanted something unique—he wanted to offer a chauffeur service that would make his venture unique and more profitable. By asking himself dozens of questions about his venture and how he could improve service, he came up with the answer: use antique cars to chauffeur his clients around.

Kenny developed the idea further by purchasing a partially restored 1931 Chrysler Imperial 8 and finishing the restoration. He then contacted antique car clubs in the area and offered to pay them 34 percent of his chauffeur service fee if he used their car. Seven old cars were signed up on a reservation basis—from a 1916 Model T to a 1953 Studebaker Starlite Coupe—and Kenny made a small flyer with photos for his unique chauffeur service.

Today, Kenny's venture covers a three state area plus Washington, D.C. Classic Chauffeur Service owns six classic and antique cars and has eleven more on call. Kenny learned how to not only choose and operate his own Weekend Wealth Venture, but also how to make it unique and profitable.

PINPOINTING YOUR PROFITS

To have the greatest control of your costs and profits, you need to know exactly what each unit or hour you produce has cost and how much you can earn with it. If you're selling a product, you'll want to know what each unit cost you to make and how much you can expect to make with it. If you're selling a service, you'll break down your costs and profit into hours.

Here are the things you'll need to know to estimate your costs and profit per unit/hour:

- Raw materials: What are the costs of the components of my product before I turn them into the finished product I sell?

- Overhead: What ongoing costs do I have for office or working space, lights, heat, phone, office supplies, that I must pass on to my customers?
- Labor: How much is my own labor worth per hour? Will I hire others? At what cost (including payroll taxes)?
- Promotion: How much will it cost me to advertise and promote my product or service to potential customers? How much per unit/hour?
- Return on investment: How much would a bank give me if I were to deposit my capital in a savings account? This is also an expense of operation.
- Total costs: What are my total costs to produce and distribute my product or service? How much will it sell for? What is my profit per unit or hour sold?

How Ruth A. Earns Hundreds of Dollars Each Month In Her Spare Time

Ruth A. chose a secretarial service as her Weekend Wealth Venture. Working in an office during the day, Ruth had both the skills to build her venture and a healthy respect for accounting principles. She decided to make her enterprise profitable from the first day by discovering her profit per hour.

Ruth estimated the costs of raw materials (paper and supplies), overhead (partial rent on her apartment, cost of typewriter and Dictaphone), labor (at $5 an hour for herself as her one and only employee), promotion (a small classified ad), distribution (mailing costs), return on investment (5½ percent interest on her $300 investment), and total costs per hour ($8).

Ruth then estimated production as typing 70 words per minute. At this speed she could finish about 16 double-spaced pages an hour. She decided that if she offered to type them at the going rate in her area of 75 cents a double-spaced page she would be earning an income of $12 an hour. That gave Ruth a profit—after her own salary as employee—of $4 hour.

Ruth now offers a more unique secretarial service in Sacramento, California. She takes jobs and estimates them at $12 an hour, then gives them to other part time typists who do the work at $9 an hour. She profits a full $3 an hour per subcontractor—which means that when she has five typists working on the jobs that she brings in for them, Ruth is making $15 an hour without touching the keyboard.

Ruth earns more with her part-time venture than with her full-time job—and works much less—because she discovered exactly how much it costs to offer her venture to others and how much she profits from it. Ruth now shares her profits with other typists who do the work for her. Ruth is clearly a smart Weekend Wealth Builder.

FIVE WAYS TO MULTIPLY VENTURE PROFITS EFFICIENTLY

By now you're ready to learn and use advanced techniques for adding extra profit dollars to your venture with these proven steps:

* Improve purchasing - Start researching new and less costly sources for the equipment and supplies you most use in your venture. One simple source could easily double your profits. Check with other entrepreneurs and in the phone book for products you buy.

* Better distribution - Look at alternative methods of getting your product or service to your customer efficiently. Look for a quicker or less costly delivery service, using the phone instead of the mails, using a parcel delivery service or other methods.

* Increase sales - Once you've discovered your cost per unit/hour and built in a healthy profit per unit/hour, it's time to increase sales and develop new markets for your product or service. More on this profitable step later.

* Standardize - You can add many extra profit dollars to your venture by standardizing your methods of operation. You can set up an assembly line for prod-

ucts you produce. You can develop forms and question lists to increase efficiency in your service.

* Keep good records - A complete record system will help you make extra money by pointing to highly profitable areas in your venture as well as low-profit activities. This will be discussed further in Chapter 11.

You'll read more about this dynamic five-point system for increasing Venture Profits in the coming pages.

BRINGING PROFITABLE NEW CUSTOMERS TO YOUR DOORSTEP

There are basically two types of distribution systems:

* Your customers come to you to buy
* You go to your customers to sell

The advantage to having buyers come to you is that you save on distribution costs. On the other hand, the advantage of going directly to them to sell is that you can more closely control how much business you do. You don't have to wait for them to come to you and buy.

Your distribution or marketing system depends a lot on the Weekend Wealth Venture you build. As a newsletter publisher you go to your customers to make the sale via the mails. If you operated a part-time snow cone stand, your customers would come to your location.

Even so, there are things you can do as an intelligent Weekend Wealth Builder to build your profits by reaching more potential customers when you most want them. I'll illustrate this point by showing you—

How Sam B. Built His Venture With Found Customers

Sam B. knew a little about marketing before he chose bicycle repair as his Weekend Wealth Venture. He knew that, for the most part, he would have to depend on customers who came to him. Here's how he built his part time business with smart marketing:

* *Find them* - Sam decided that his customers would be bicycle riders in Ogden, Utah, who needed repairs to their bikes. He found the greatest concentration of them along city bike paths and within two area bike clubs.

* *Tell them* - To reach these bikers with his service and motivate them to come to him for repairs, Sam made signs much like the roadside Burma Shave signs of a few decades ago and set them up along the paths: *When your bike/Needs Repairs/See the man/Who really cares/Sam's Bike Shop*. He also offered a ten percent discount to members of area bike clubs.

* *Service them* - Finally, Sam made sure that his best advertisement was from satisfied customers. They soon spread the word and Sam's weekend and evening bike repair shop was earning him as much as his regular job in a clothing store.

Sam knew how to bring profitable customers to him and keep them coming back. Sam is a successful and very rich Weekend Wealth Builder.

GOING WHERE THE BIG MONEY IS

Many other types of Weekend Wealth Ventures require that you take your product or service to where the customer is—in his home, car, at recreation or at work. Here's how the smart entrepreneur finds new customers and new profits quickly:

* *Door-to-door* - Lloyd A. built weekend profits by going to the wholesale flower market on Saturday mornings and buying carnations and roses by the dozen. He then wrapped them in half-dozen packages, drove through residential neighborhoods and sold them to old and new customers. Profits: $50 to $150 per Saturday.

* *Telephone* - Jerry N.'s service was unique. He helped owners of condominiums in resort areas book renters during the off season by phone. Jerry called professional people both at work and at home and offered the use of resort condos at off-season rates. Jerry's commission was 20 percent and he often made $200 a day helping others save money on their vacations by telephone.

* *Shows, fairs, gatherings* - Linda C. set up her small travel trailer wherever large groups of people gathered, and sold fast food. She put a grill in her galley, used the refrigerator for cold drinks and put up folding tables and chairs under the trailer's awning. Linda took her weekend fast food wagon to Little League baseball fields, art shows, craft fairs, flea marts and other gatherings. She ran the grill while her 15-year-old daughter took orders and collected the money.

* *Mail order* - Joanne S. built her worthwhile venture completely through the mails. She knew that there were thousands of lonely people who were looking for companionship through letters. Joanne started Pen Pals International, offering a monthly bulletin listing new members interested in corresponding with others. Her venture gives her an extra $300 to $400 a month—plus the satisfaction of helping hundreds of unseen customers throughout the world.

GETTING OTHERS TO BUILD YOUR VENTURE

Many smart Weekend Wealth Builders have learned that they can multiply their profits by hiring professional sales people to sell their product or service on a commission basis—no sales, no pay.

Using sales representatives will not only free you for administrative and production duties, it will also bring you greater profits through efficiency. Your salesman will be working in a larger market than you may be able to reach simply because that's his full-time job.

Here's how venture operators find and profit from representatives:

* *Contact* - You'll find professional sales representatives in many places: in trade and sales magazine ads, in your local phone book and among friends and acquaintances.
* *Determine Qualifications* - To make sure they are qualified and productive enough to help you sell your part time venture's product or service, ask them what they have to offer you, how much they charge, how they will sell your product and how much they realistically expect to sell each month? Their answers will help you hire the most productive—and honest—on a straight commission basis.
* *Help Sell* - Once you've hired a sales representative to find buyers for your product or service, help him sell for you by stocking him with necessary information, literature, and sales aids. Answer his questions and help him understand the product or service he's selling.

A smart Weekend Wealth Builder often distributes his product or service through profitable sales representatives to increase his income with less time.

How Gary E. Discovered The Right Rep For His Venture

Gary E. of Lakewood, Ohio, built the perfect Weekend Wealth Venture for him in his garage. Using large plaster molds purchased in a going-out-of-business sale, Gary made lawn decorations and sold them through a nearby building materials store.

One day, Gary was bringing in a load of plaster ducks, fountains and figurines when a wholesale hardware salesman spotted him and asked him about his merchandise. Over coffee, Gary and the rep talked about Gary's enterprise. How many could he produce? How much does he sell them for, wholesale? Would he like to expand his venture? How much? The rep offered to represent Gary's firm to other building material firms he called on. Gary asked him how many he felt he could sell, could he get more to cover the increased cost of sales, and what his fee would be.

They soon made a deal. Today, Gary operates his plaster lawn decoration venture full-time. Of course, he's now letting employees do the menial work while he spends time at the helm of his profitable business—and his new motorhome. Gary quickly learned how to put others to work making profits for him with the Weekend Wealth Plan. Gary uses the Power of Dynamic Motivation.

EXPLOITING OTHER PROFIT PRODUCERS

There are many other ways you can market and distribute your venture's product or service. Here are three of the most popular—and profitable.

- Direct mail campaigns
- Drop-ship representatives
- Newspaper/magazine ads

Harry C. of Minneapolis used all three to build his highly profitable disc jockey correspondence school. With six years of experience in radio, Harry decided to capitalize on his knowledge; he set up a 20-lesson course for aspiring radio announcers and supplemented it with a tape evaluation service.

To build his part-time venture, Harry developed a brief, but powerful pamphlet on the field of radio and how his school operated—ten dollars per lesson in advance and 20 dollars for a written critique on voice tapes sent to him for evaluation. The literature was sent by direct mail to radio stations across the nation, as well as to people who answered small ads that Harry placed in youth-oriented magazines.

Finally, Harry advertised for agents in other parts of the country, offering them exclusive right to sell his course in their area. He charged dealers five dollars a lesson and ten dollars for the critique—half the retail price—dropshipped. That is, when they sold the lesson, they kept five dollars and sent the other five in with the order and Harry mailed the lesson directly to the customer. As future lessons were ordered, Harry got five dollars and the representative received five dollars.

Harry's part-time enterprise earned him a healthy $12,000 last year. Harry used direct mail, magazine ads and drop-shipping methods to increase his income while keeping costs down. Harry is a smart Weekend Wealth Builder.

HOW OTHER SMART ENTREPRENEURS SUCCESSFULLY PRODUCED AND MARKETED THEIR VENTURES

The opportunities for building extra profits through advanced techniques are as limitless as your imagination. You can join these and other successful Weekend Wealth Builders and enjoy greater profits and satisfaction by using the techniques you've learned in this chapter. Here are a few more smart operators:

* *Ray M.* painted homes on the weekend. He earned an extra $100 to $300 each weekend, but he was looking for even more income. Using the Weekend Wealth Plan, Ray found other Weekend Wealth Builders with painting skills, found house painting jobs for them and pocketed a 20 percent fee for lining up the jobs. He helped himself as he helped others. Ray knew how to reach new customers and sell more service at greater profits.

* *Eva T.* made pies on the weekends and sold them to restaurants in Rapid City, South Dakota. By keeping good records, Eva soon learned that three pies were more popular than the others: blackberry, French apple and rhubarb. She decided that she could increase her productivity and cut costs by specializing in these three types. She was right. Eva's Homemade Pies are offered in nearly every restaurant in the area—and Eva makes a healthy profit on each because she kept records and learned which product sold the best.

YOU CAN MULTIPLY PROFITS WITH
THE POWER OF DYNAMIC MOTIVATION

You've discovered—and started—your profitable Weekend Wealth Venture. Congratulations! You're on your road to extra cash in your spare time with the Weekend Wealth Plan.

You've learned how to develop a wide market for your venture and quickly estimate your profits per unit or hour sold.

You've learned how to discover new customers and bring them to you—or go to them—profitably,

You've also seen how smart Weekend Wealth Builders employ others to help them market their products or service for extra profits.

You've uncovered the secrets of many smart opportunity seekers who have traded a few spare hours and everyday talents for rewarding cash with the Weekend Wealth Plan. You're on the road to success.

ENERGIZING YOUR WEEKEND WEALTH PLAN

The Power of Dynamic Motivation can help you turn a simple opportunity into a wealth-building spare time venture. You can profitably produce and distribute your venture's product or service by following these easy steps right now:

1. Develop dynamic uses for your product or service. Ask yourself: What will this be used for? How can it best fill its intended need for my customers? What other uses could it be put to? What is the value of my product or service to others?

2. Pinpoint your profits by quickly estimating your costs and profits per unit/hour. Find your cost of raw materials, overhead, labor, promotion, distribution and a return on your investment. Know how much you will profit from each unit you produce or each hour you offer for sale.

3. Discover new ways of bringing customers to your doorstep. Reread this chapter and learn how to find them, sell them and service them profitably.

4. Go where the big money is with unique methods of distribution used by other smart Weekend Wealth Builders. Expand your venture by selling door-to-door, over the phone, at shows, fairs and other gatherings, through mail order or through commission sales representatives.

5. Review advanced techniques of building your venture through direct mail campaigns, drop-ship representatives and newspaper/magazine ads profitably.

Weekend Wealth Building Techniques That Quickly Overcome And Neutralize Competition

One of the most successful Weekend Wealth Builders I met in my research for this book, Don D. of Scranton, Pennsylvania, told me:

The key to part-time riches is not in developing a unique enterprise, but in offering it to the people who can best use it. Much of my own wealth came from promoting my venture profitably.

Don operates a highly successful handwriting analysis venture through the mails and actually makes more with his Weekend Wealth Venture than he does with his full-time job as a bank loan officer.

How Don and a dozen other successful venture builders market and promote their businesses is the topic of this chapter. No matter what your own chosen part-time venture is—no matter how uniquely you've developed it—you'll be able to multiply your profits quickly as you learn how smart Weekend Wealth Builders discover new profit dollars with the Weekend Wealth Plan.

PROFIT ACCELERATORS FOR PART-TIME WEALTH BUILDERS

As you learn and understand the basic concepts of my Weekend Wealth Plan, you can be offered new and advanced techniques for building Profit Accelerators. You're now ready to grasp many of these advanced techniques and use them in your own venture to build extra profits the easy way.

In this chapter, you'll discover the Market Chain, your own Target Customer and how to best reach him with your idea. You'll see how other successful venture builders have used a few basic principles to multiply their part-time income many times while decreasing the amount of time they must devote to their profit enterprise.

You'll also discover techniques for promoting your venture to the right people. You'll learn how to save thousands of dollars in advertising. You'll find out how to get free advertising for your product or service. You'll discover the secrets of getting immediate results from your advertising dollar.

You're going to uncover dozens of Profit Accelerators illustrated by successful Weekend Wealth Builders. Any one of these techniques could be the one that leads you to greater wealth and satisfaction with your own profit opportunity.

FINDING YOUR LINK IN THE MARKET CHAIN

There are four simple steps in the Market Chain that takes a product or service to the consumer profitably:

Producer
        Wholesaler
                Retailer
                        Consumer

The Producer develops and builds the product, then sells it in large quantity to distributors or Wholesalers and takes his profit. The Wholesaler then sells lesser quantities to many Retailers and takes his profit from the transaction. Next, the Retailer sells the product individually to the Consumer for a profit. For the convenience of purchasing the product in a quantity he can use, the Consumer pays an indirect profit to both the Retailer and the Wholesaler—middlemen in the Market Chain.

Here's how smart Weekend Wealth Builders use this knowledge of the Market Chain to build extra profits for themselves:

* *Combining steps* - Many fortunes are made by those who eliminate one or more of the middlemen and sell directly to the ultimate Consumer. The Producer may decide to sell his product as a factory outlet directly to the Consumer and pocket the profits of the Wholesaler and Retailer. The Wholesaler may also be the Retailer and pass part of the savings on to the Consumer. There are many profitable variations on the Market Chain.

* *Adding steps* - You can also find profits by adding steps to the Market Chain. You may find a major Producer in another country, buy directly from him and sell to Wholesalers in this country. You can also profit from stepping between the Wholesaler and Retailers to buy a product in quantity and sell it in smaller quantities more useable and profitable to Retailers.

There are thousands of dollars in part-time profits that can be banked by the smart Weekend Wealth Builder who knows how the system operates and where the profits are.

How Nell H. Discovered Extra Profits In The Market Chain

Nell H. of Tucson, Arizona, was selling a small but useful booklet directly to the Consumer when she discovered the profits available in the Market Chain. Her booklet, *Free Publications Directory*, offered sources for over 200 books, booklets, magazines and newsletters that were available from business and government simply for the asking. The booklet sold for two dollars.

By adding another step between her, the Producer, and the Consumer, Nell was able to increase her sales and profits. Working as her own Wholesaler, Nell found a number of Retailers, new mail order businessmen, who would buy her booklet for one dollar and resell it for two dollars and more. Of course, her profit per transaction was cut almost in half, but her total sales quickly multiplied by 1700 percent.

To build her Weekend Wealth Venture profits, Nell simply added a link to the Market Chain and expanded her potential income.

DISCOVERING YOUR TARGET CUSTOMER FOR INCREASED PROFITS

You can also multiply your venture's income by finding out who your typical or Target Customer is and taking steps to reach him profitably.

To make this valuable discovery, ask yourself:

* Who would buy my product or service?
* What needs do they want satisfied?
* How are those needs being satisfied now?
* How can I improve on similar products and services offered?
* How can I easily reach my Target Customer to tell him about my product or service?
* What newspapers and magazines does he read? How often?

* Does he live in a certain neighborhood or city? A particular part of the country?
* Do I know someone who is a likely Target Customer? Can I interview him?
* Am I my own Target Customer? If so, how could someone reach me to tell me of his product or service?

The smart Weekend Wealth Builder will try to discover his Target Customer, find out how to reach him with his message and benefits, then sell him.

How Gerold K. Found Thousands Of Dollars In Profits With His Target Customer

Gerold K. is a happily married man who decided he wanted to offer his family more of the "Good Life" while building a part-time enterprise. Gerold found the right Weekend Wealth Venture for him—one that showed tremendous potential in his area—a messenger-courier service.

Just before he started his one-man enterprise, Gerold organized the search for his Target Customer and how to best tell him of his venture. He decided that his Target Customer would have these traits:

- He would be a businessman in California's San Fernando Valley
- He would have a need for a package or message to be quickly relayed to a customer or other businessman.
- He would want prompt, efficient and honest service at his convenience.
- He would have three messenger-courier services to choose from in his area—none of which offered service on the weekends
- His Target Customer reads the phone book yellow pages, the *Valley Advertiser* newspaper and direct mail literature
- He can call on Target Customers and confirm their needs, desires and motivation to insure his venture's success

Defining his Target Customer gave Gerold two separate opportunities:

1. To operate his messenger-courier service only on the weekends, either independently or in conjunction with a venture someone else is operating weekdays, or

2. To operate his messenger-courier service full-time—having his older son make weekday afternoon pickups and deliveries while he made weekend runs.

Gerold chose number two. It not only builds his own income, but also offers his son, a college student, the opportunity to work his way through Valley State College. After that, Gerold has two other children who can help him earn extra money. Gerold's messenger service is a highly successful—and profitable—venture because he defined his Target Customer and decided on the best way to reach him.

QUICK PROFIT METHODS OF SELLING YOUR TARGET CUSTOMER

Once you have identified and reached your Target Customer, you'll be ready to use advanced salesmanship techniques to persuade him to use your product or service. Here's how the Weekend Wealth Builders do it:

Salesmanship is nothing more than the art of persuasion. You can persuade people to do as you desire by using this dynamic three-step method. Try it on someone you know.

First, set your listener off balance.

Second, keep him off balance.

Third, show him how he can rebalance himself by doing as you ask.

To illustrate this dynamic method, let's see—

How Jack S. Multiplied His Profits With Dynamic Sales Techniques

Jack S. was the first one to admit it—he was no born salesman.

Even so, Jack saw the value in learning the art of persuasion, so he began studying it and how he could use it in developing his Weekend Wealth Venture: stamp trading. Here's how he applied this dynamic three-step system to convince a customer that he needed a particular stamp more than he needed the money it took to purchase it:

Off Balance	Don, your stamp collection just won't be complete without this addition.
Keep Off Balance	Not only will this stamp be an investment that will increase in value—it will also complete your set and increase the value of your entire collection. In fact, your set is worth less than it could be because you don't have it.
Help Rebalance	The cost of this stamp— twelve dollars—is much less than its value. And to make it easy for you to buy it, I'll take just half now and half next week. That's fair, isn't it?

See how it works? You've probably seen professional salesmen use this technique on you and others around you. It's very effective in helping your customers make the best decision for them—using your product or service.

Jack soon overcame his fear of sales and built his stamp trading business to a $200 to $300 a week venture he operated during his lunch hour at the auto factory where he worked. Jack enjoyed persuading people to fulfill his wishes.

PROMOTING VENTURE PROFITS

That's how it works. That's how the smart Weekend Wealth Builders market their products and services. They choose the most profitable link in the Market Chain, learn all they can about their Target Customer, decide on the best way to reach him, then use dynamic persuasion methods to sell him.

Now it's time to discover new Profit Accelerators—how to promote your Weekend Wealth Venture to the widest number of Target Customers profitably.

To promote means to increase. The laws of promotion will help you to *increase* both Target Customer awareness of your product or service and your own profits. You can promote your venture with a big dollar promotional and advertising campaign—or you can use my Weekend Wealth Plan to promote your venture economically.

I'm sure you've chosen the latter.

To effectively promote your Weekend Wealth Venture you must use what you've learned about your Target Customer, your venture, and persuasion to come up with a simple message about your product or service. Once you have it, you must get that message in front of the right people often enough to convince them to try your product or service. Finally, promotion of your venture means measuring the response you get from each of your efforts to see which is most effective.

How Mark S. Promoted Himself Profitably

Mark S. operates a successful import business in Miami, Florida. Mark says that one of the biggest things that made it successful was what he learned about the power of promotion and how to effectively use it.

When he first started his venture three years ago, Mark was importing small transistor radios that received the National Weather Service's radio frequencies. They gave the listeners up-to-date weather forecasts day and night.

Mark used the powers of marketing and promotion to discover and sell his Target Customer. He knew he had a wide clientele—if he could reach them inexpensively. Mark knew that everyone who lived in Florida and the Gulf Coast states was a Target Customer for a weather radio that told them of hurricanes and storms in advance. The problem was reaching them at a cost that allowed him a healthy profit on the imported radios.

Mark used the techniques for securing free advertising that you'll soon learn about, to make millions of people aware of his product and its value. His message to them was persuasive. Within six weeks, Mark had received orders for over 1100 weather radios at $14.95 each. His profit was over $6,600. Why so much? Because he discovered his Target Customer and aimed right for him with persuasive and effective messages.

Mark is a very smart—and very rich—Weekend Wealth Builder.

MAKING BIG MONEY WITH THE POWER OF ADVERTISING

Advertising is simply promoting something to the public. But the Power of Advertising is much more. It's the power to gain attention, interest, desire and action of a wide group of people through mass persuasion.

Here's how successful Weekend Wealth Builders increase their income with the Power of Advertising:

* *Response ads* - Many ads are aimed at persuading the reader to act—to respond to the message. If the product or service is one that can be explained and promoted easily, smart advertisers use response ads that will directly bring orders.

* *Attitude ads* - If your product or service is one that's difficult to describe in print and you must face the Target Customer in order to sell him, try attitude ads. These ads make generalizations about low prices, better service, more convenience or other benefits, then encourage readers or listeners to come and see you for more details.

The smart Weekend Wealth Builders have also learned that, generally, the print media—newspapers, magazines, mail-out literature—are best for response ads, and that the broadcast media—radio and television—are best for attitude ads where a positive image rather than facts sell your product or service.

To see how the Power of Advertising is put to work by successful venture operators, let's see—

How Terry N. Cut Advertising Costs In Half Quickly

Terry N. knew he was spending too much money on advertising, but he also knew he had to in order to bring in enough customers for his wedding photo service. He thought that if he cut back on his advertising he would lose business.

One day he came to me for business advice. I counseled him on the Power of Advertising and he discovered that he was using the wrong type of ads for his venture. He was using large ads in the local newspaper to build the *image* of wedding photography. Many readers were sold on the *idea* of having photos made of their wedding, then grabbed a phone book or saw another ad that earned their response. Terry's ad campaign was actually giving his competition more business.

We quickly changed Terry's ad campaign. He still used an image-building photo of a wedding to arouse the reader's interest, but Terry went further by working toward a response from readers. He offered a "limited time only" photo album and two extra photos for friends or relatives free of charge. Terry earned their quick response. We also cut Terry's ad budget in half.

Results? Terry's wedding photo service now does nearly twice as much business with half the advertising costs. His ads are more effective. Also, when they ask for the free album, Terry knows that the Target Customer came from his new advertising campaign.

Terry knows how to use the Power of Advertising profitably.

LOCATING AND USING SOURCES OF FREE ADVERTISING

How would you like to increase your Weekend Wealth Venture profits and multiply your customers with free advertising and promotion. Sure you would. You've seen what the Power of Advertising can do and, if you can get it for free, all the better.

Here are three powerful ways of getting free advertising for your product or service:

* *Word-Of-Mouth Advertising* - The greatest and least expensive advertising of all. Word-of-mouth advertising comes from satisfied customers who say good things about your product or service. Encourage your customers' satisfaction and promotion. It is the most believable and least costly form of advertising you have.

* *Publicity Releases* - Other forms of free advertising are stories in newspapers and magazines that tell about your product or service. They may be on a new product you offer, a unique use of your product or service, an article on how to use it safely and effectively, or other publicity. They can be written by you or a professional publicist and sent to area newspapers, magazines and broadcast stations.

* *Newsworthy Events* - A smart Weekend Wealth Builder can often gain free advertising by sponsoring a local event; by giving an interview about the fun and foibles of being an independent businessman; of marking the anniversary of your venture, the invention of your product or other newsworthy event. If you feel you have a newsworthy story, contact your local radio station or newspaper. Sell them on your idea and you may get thousands of dollars worth of free advertising with little effort.

Rod A. of Cincinnati, Ohio, offers a good example of how to earn free advertising for your Weekend Wealth Venture. Rod offered a resumé service that wrote and produced job resumés for people looking for employment. To publicize his name, Rod contacted an editor at the *Cleveland Plain Dealer* about a unique news story.

The following Sunday, Rod had a full-page story about his business on the front page of the local features section. The illustrated feature told readers about two things:

1. How to best search for a new job, and
2. Unusual resumés Rod has helped write

Without giving names, Rod candidly talked about the many unique resumés for circus performers, a pet cemetery salesman, a movie stuntman and a private detective who specialized in lost husbands. It made interesting reading—and gave Rod free advertising that he could never afford to buy.

From this full page "ad," Rod received recognition as an expert at helping others find jobs through resumés. He soon had more business than he could handle on his days off from his regular job at a trucking company. He had to quit his job and take the resumé service on full-time—and he doubled his old salary. Rod says he owes it all to his free advertising campaign.

GETTING BIG RESULTS FOR YOUR VENTURE PROMOTION

The purpose of your advertising and promotion campaign is to turn Target Customers iinto paying customers. You want results. Here's how the most successful Weekend Wealth Builders in the nation turn people on and get them to buy from them:

* *Use your customers* - Smart operators use their current customers to attract new customers by offering discounts to those who send him business, by asking about friends who may be interested in his product or service and contacting them, and by giving them business cards and asking them to give them to friends and acquaintances.

* *Key your ads and promotion* - Once you've started an advertising or promotion campaign, develop some

system for distinguishing the source of each customer. If you're running ads for orders to be sent to a post office box number, have one ad read "Box 437-A," another one "Box 437-B" and so forth. Then keep track of how many responses you received from each ad and decide why each succeeded or failed. By keying ads you'll quickly discover the best way to promote your venture profitably.

* *Special give-aways* - Everyone likes something for nothing. You can both increase and measure promotion results with a giveaway. With an ad for a product you can offer a "free bonus product with each order." If you offer a service, you can offer the first hour, day or week of service free to new customers who sign up now. You'll attract new customers and also be able to discover how they learned about your venture.

That's how the smart Weekend Wealth Builders insure profitable results for their advertising campaigns—paid or free. Follow their lead to a successful ad campaign.

14 WAYS TO PROMOTE PROFITS

As a special bonus to this chapter, here are 14 revealing questions you can use to lead you to greater income through venture promotion.

* Can you describe your product's or service's benefits in two minutes or less?
* Is one time of the year better for promoting your venture than another? Why?
* Will some of your suppliers help you with cooperative advertising and pay part of the ad bill?
* Is there one special feature that can help sell your product or service easier?
* Can customers buy from you on credit?
* Do you accept major credit cards?
* Do you offer a free delivery service?
* Do you send a letter to old customers every few months?

* Where is the best place to promote your venture?
* Can you promote your Weekend Wealth Venture through your regular job?
* Do you make it easier for your customers to say "yes" than "no"?
* Are there trade shows, exhibits or flea markets in your area where you can reach more Target Customers at one time?
* Can you offer a "full money-back guarantee" on your product or service to promote good will and future business?
* Are there trade organizations in your field that can help you in promoting your venture?

YOU CAN SUCCESSFULLY MARKET AND PROMOTE YOUR WEEKEND WEALTH VENTURE FOR PROFIT

Your Weekend Wealth Venture is well along the road to success. To accelerate its progress—and to insure you of greater profits—you've learned how to quickly take your venture to the people who can best use it.

You've learned how to successfully market your product or service in the Market Chain. You've discovered your own Target Customer and learned how to profitably reach him. Then you've learned how to put dynamic sales techniques to work to convince him of the value of your opportunity.

You've also discovered how to increase income without increasing expenses with free advertising. You've learned about the difference between response ads and attitude ads—and which ones to use in your venture. You have discovered new sources of free advertising and seen how to put them to work for you. Finally, you have found new ways to get greater results from your promotion campaign—and turn your weekends into wealth.

You have the knowledge—and the motivation—to promote your venture profitably.

ENERGIZING YOUR WEEKEND WEALTH PLAN

You can quickly overcome and neutralize competition for your Target Customer's dollar by using the advanced profit techniques for marketing and promoting your venture as outlined in this chapter. To activate your plan, do these things right now:

1. Find your own link in the Market Chain. Are you a Producer, Wholesaler, Retailer or one of the links in between? Can you combine or add steps to the Chain for increased profits? Do it.

2. Discover your own Target Customer and use my three-step system for selling him.

3. Promote your venture with response ads, attitude ads and free advertising techniques. List four sources for profitable promotion of your Weekend Wealth Venture.

4. Get results for your promotion and advertising campaigns by following the simple steps in this chapter: use your customers, key your ads, and offer special giveaways. Can you think of other profitable ways?

5. Review the 14 Ways to Promote Increased Profits and come up with at least six that you can apply to your venture now.

Controlling Others To Multiply Weekend Wealth Venture Profits

Many people are ready and anxious to help you make big money with your spare time enterprise—if you know how to "turn them on."

That's right. The Weekend Wealth Plan offers the power to control others and have them develop extra profit dollars in your behalf.

Sound good? It's great! Hundreds of smart Weekend Wealth Builders are this minute applying the simple techniques you'll soon learn, to build their ventures the easy way. You can follow their clear example. You can apply the steps they developed. You can learn from their success.

You must not abuse this power. You must use it only for the common good of you *and* your customers and employees. You must use this power responsibly.

Ready?

Here's one of the most exciting discoveries you'll make on your road to Weekend Wealth.

CREATING PLUS-PROFITS WITH THE POWER OF MOTIVATION

One of the greatest techniques of the Weekend Wealth Plan is the *Power of Motivation.* It's the power over others to make them work for you. The Power of Motivation will show you:

* How to earn extra dollars by turning more prospects into profitable customers
* How to discover what each customer is looking for and how to help him find it
* How to motivate employees and other business contacts to work harder for your venture
* How to turn on suppliers and have them give you their best prices and terms
* How to build new markets for your venture and turn them into extra cash
* How to motivate bankers to offer you unlimited funds

You can even apply this power to other parts of your life. You can motivate family and friends to do things for you. You can motivate your full-time employer to promote you and give you more pay. You can use this dynamic power in your contacts with public officials, sales clerks, neighbors, fellow employees and others who have an effect on your life.

MASTERING THE POWER OF MOTIVATION

The Power of Motivation is the *power to discover and use a common incentive for mutual satisfaction*. That is, you must find out what the person you're dealing with wants, then show him how he can get it in exchange for what you desire.

The Power of Motivation is in constant use by successful people. Here are some examples you'll recognize:

* A television commercial motivates viewers to trade protection againt "ring around the collar" for the purchase price of Wisk.
* A minister tells his congregation about the blessing they will receive in exchange for money for the missions.
* A city official motivates constituents to reelect him by promising that things they want to have done will be done.
* A salesman explains the benefits of the latest model car to an interested prospect.

See how it works? The Power of Motivation makes you think of what your adversary wants before you can make a trade with him. Once he wants what he has (money) less that what he desires (your product or service), a sale is made.

How Paul E. Discovered The Power Of Motivation

Paul E. of Indianapolis, Indiana, had a problem that was holding him back from success. His Weekend Wealth Venture, a window washing service, just wasn't attracting enough customers to be profitable.

Paul made a market study before he started his venture and he knew that there were thousands of potential customers, but he just couldn't get them to sign up for his service. He was ready to throw in the towel when he finally talked with a prominent business consultant about his problem.

The consultant quickly found the solution.

Paul had been telling prospects why he needed their business—not the other way around. He said, "I have six years of experience as a window cleaner. I have a van to carry my equipment around from job to job. I am on call on my days off: Wednesday and Sunday." The consultant explained that his prospects don't really care about his equipment—they only want to know how what he offers will benefit them.

Paul now tells his prospects:

> *You'll have the brightest, shiniest windows in town because I have the experience and equipment to do a better job than anyone else.*
>
> *You can choose either midweek or weekend service–whichever is convenient for you.*
>
> *You can save even more money on necessary window washing service by approving a one-year contract tailored to your needs.*

The results? Paul's window washing service now gives him an extra $300 to $400 a month—because he used the Power of Motivation to turn his customers on profitably.

PUTTING THE POWER OF MOTIVATION TO WORK IN YOUR WEEKEND WEALTH VENTURE

The Power of Motivation can often spell the difference between a small income and a great and growing income. All you have to do is put it to work in your own spare time enterprise. Here's my four-step plan for applying the Power of Motivation:

* Decide what you want to have done
* Decide who would best do it for you
* Discover how to motivate that person to act
* Use the Power of Motivation to reach your goal

Examples are the best teachers so let's see how one smart Weekend Wealth Builder put the Power of Motivation into action for herself.

Kathy S. was a secretary in a large law firm when she decided to turn her spare time and talents into extra cash. She decided to start a stenographic service for lawyers in her home town of Eugene, Oregon. She added a different twist to her venture—Kathy offered to take shorthand by phone in the evening hours. Lawyers could call her at home between seven and eleven p.m., dictate a letter, and have it typed and delivered to their offices by nine a.m. the next morning.

She needed to get the word out to lawyers so she used my four-step plan to accomplish her publicity campaign like this:

To be done: Have influential lawyers offer word-of-mouth advertising for my service.

Who should do: Miles T., member of many local legal associations and influential in the legal profession in Eugene.

How to motivate: Explain the service to him and build his ego by asking his advice on how best to reach the legal community. Also ask him to be first trial customer.

Do it: Kathy called Miles and told him, "I know that you're one of the busiest and most influential attorneys in the area and I need your help. Most successful lawyers work long hours and often need to dictate letters in the evenings for the next day's mail. I'm sure you do, don't you? I'd like you to be my first customer, at no charge, in exchange for your telling me how I can offer the most useful evening steno service to other members of your profession. Your advice and assistance would be very helpful."

Miles was flattered. After a trial period and a few suggestions, Kathy launched her evening steno service with Miles' help. He told his partners about the service and even publicized it in the state's bulletin. Soon, Kathy had more business than she could handle in the evenings and hired another legal secretary to take some of her calls on a percentage basis. Kathy now often earns as much in the evenings as she does in her daytime job. She's a smart Weekend Wealth Builder who knows how to put the Power of Motivation into action to get things done.

MULTIPLYING CUSTOMERS WITH BUYER MOTIVATION

The most important people to you as a Weekend Wealth Builder are your customers. These are the people you most want to motivate. You want them to buy from you. Here's how you can use the Power of Motivation to turn prospects into profitable customers.

First, discover why your customers would want to buy from you. Ask yourself:

* What need does my prospect have for my product or service? How strong is this need? Slight? Great? Average?

* What about desire? Is this something that my prospect would like to have to improve his style of life? Will it fulfill this desire?

* Can my prospect justify the cost of my product or service as compared to other needs and costs in his life? How does it compare with similar products and services offered to my prospect by others?

* How can I best motivate my prospect to make the right decision—for himself and for me? What will make him want the product more than he wants the money it will take to purchase it?

The first three points are preliminary questions leading up to the fourth point: How can I motivate my prospect to decide on my behalf? Smart Weekend Wealth Builders have discovered that they can turn on their prospects and help them make the right decision by discovering their "Buyer Buttons." Buyer Buttons are ideas, images, messages and thoughts that can be transferred to customers to turn them on to your product or service.

How Ed J. Discovered Buyer Buttons—And Extra Profits

Ed J. was an amateur photographer. He worked the swing shift handling air freight for one of the major airlines at the New Orleans airport, but his first love was photography. One day, Ed decided to cash in on his hobby and turn it into a profitable Weekend Wealth Venture with the Power of Motivation and the discovery of his Buyer Buttons.

First, Ed asked himself: Who are my potential customers and what need do they have for my service? Since Ed decided to specialize in photographing memorable events such as high school championship sports, local car races, local beauty contests and other events, he decided that his prospects were average people who became short-term local celebrities. Ed knew that their desire for photos of this once-in-a-lifetime event would be great.

Next, Ed set up his pricing system in line with what he felt his excited prospects would be willing to pay for his photos of their day in the limelight. He set prices at ten dollars for an 8×10 black and white photo and 15 dollars for color.

Then, Ed looked for the best way to motivate his prospects to buy from him—he searched for their Buyer Buttons. He knew that pride was the major motivation for his prospects to buy photos of their important moments.

Finally, Ed decided how to put pride motivation into his sales presentation. He got names and addresses of participants at events he covered, contacted them by phone and reminded them of the thrill they enjoyed in winning. Then he mentioned that he was a photographer and that he had a few photos of the event, and asked if they would like to see them. They always did. He made an appointment for the coming weekend and took the photos to their home. They were "turned on" by Buyer Buttons and Ed sold most of his photos at a large profit. In fact, Ed often earned 200 dollars or more in a single weekend by offering people photos of their special moments. Ed is a successful—and prosperous—Weekend Wealth Builder.

TURNING ON EMPLOYEES WITH THE
POWER OF MOTIVATION

As your Weekend Wealth Venture grows, you may find yourself looking for employees who can help you satisfy the needs of your customers profitably. These employees may be family members such as spouse, children or siblings—or complete strangers who have the skills you can capitalize on as a smart venture builder.

You can apply the Power of Motivation to these profit builders quickly and easily to help them build your business. You can do it with my four-step system for employee motivation:

* Discover motivation
* Develop motivation
* Reward
* Reinforce

It's as simple as that. You can turn inefficient employees into profit builders. You can multiply your income and business goodwill. You can expand your venture into a full-time enterprise with the Power of Motivation as applied to employees.

How Nadine G. Doubled Profits With Employee Motivation

Here's how Nadine G. of Memphis, Tennessee quickly built her Weekend Wealth Venture into a full-time enterprise with the Power of Motivation.

Nadine had been a model before she got married and settled down to domestic life. Within a few years, her two children were in school and Nadine was looking for a new challenge—and an opportunity to add to the family's income. She decided to return to modeling—this time as a modeling agent. She would book local models for fashion shows, advertising photography and related jobs.

Nadine's employees were the models she hired for jobs—many of them also part-timers who had been in modeling before. She knew that their motivation was much like hers: a challenge and cash. She discovered their motivation.

Then Nadine developed this motivation further by reminding her models that they can take pride in the service that they offer—and that she will help them earn good wages while she offers them new and exciting modeling assignments.

Nadine rewarded her employees by doing exactly what she told them she would do. She found them interesting modeling assignments that would challenge them while offering good fees. She rotated her models so that each had an opportunity at the most enjoyable and best paying assignments.

Finally, Nadine reinforced her employees' motivation by reminding them that she had delivered what she promised: a challenge and cash. Her models were loyal to her. Nadine knew how to turn her employees on profitably with the Power of Motivation.

NEW TECHNIQUES FOR CREATING EXTRA PROFITS

You've seen the Power of Motivation successfully applied to customers and employees. The smart Weekend Wealth Builder doesn't stop there. He knows how to apply this profitable power to make others do exactly what he wishes. He can use it to control:

* Salesmen
* Agents
* Suppliers
* Distributors
* Freight forwarders
* Public officials
* Friends
* Relatives
* Bankers

In fact, the Power of Motivation can be used to help you increase your profits through nearly everyone you come in contact with. Here are some advanced techniques used by successful Weekend Wealth Builders in promoting profits through others:

* *Share your wealth.* Pay others by their productivity to your enterprise. Rather than pay them by the hour, pay them by the amount of profits they bring to you—a percentage of your profits. You'll find increased wealth and improved relations.
* *Use your influence.* Once you've built a successful Weekend Wealth Venture, don't be afraid to use this power to encourage others to help you. Let bankers and public officials know of your successes as you ask for their help. Everyone wants to be included in success.

* *Think about the other person's goals.* Whether you're dealing with a supplier or a banker, he will have goals that he wants to reach. By realizing these goals and showing him how you can work together to meet your mutual goals, you will be using the Power of Motivation.

* *Put people in debt to you.* The smart Weekend Wealth Builder will encourage business contacts by offering favors to people who can help him build his business. It may be offering extra service or additional merchandise to others who can help you at a later date. Keep track of these extras and ask for favors back when you need them.

* *Use the Power of Motivation wisely.* You have the power to influence and even control others. Never abuse this power. Always use it for the good of common goals. You can help yourself and others toward greater profits with the Power of Motivation.

HOW OTHER SUCCESSFUL WEEKEND WEALTH BUILDERS MOTIVATE OTHERS PROFITABLY

Here are two more successful business builders who want to share their knowledge and application of the Power of Motivation with you:

* John R. depended on part-time employees to operate his venture, raising flowers for local flower shops. He had one employee who had experience in raising flowers, but he was becoming a problem—he wouldn't take direction. Using the Power of Motivation, John discovered that this employee was working part-time to build up capital to start his.own enterprise. John used this fact to find out how they could reach their common goals. After a lengthy talk, John offered to take him on as a working partner and become a silent partner in the enterprise. It worked. Today, John earns as much as he used to from his

enterprise—without the headaches. John found a way for them to reach their common goals with the Power of Motivation.

* Tom V. ran a joke service for disc jockeys and comedians. Once a month, Tom sent out a humor newsletter to subscribers in six states. He could expand his venture profitably if he had the cash for advertising and promotion so he went to his banker. Tom used the Power of Motivation to show the loan officer how they could reach their common goals through his expansion. The banker wanted a successful loan and Tom wanted a successful venture. They both reached their goals because Tom knew how to use the Power of Motivation on others.

YOU CAN MOTIVATE OTHERS PROFITABLY

The key to the Golden Circle of Wealth is in your hands. You can use the dynamic and profitable Power of Motivation to build your Weekend Wealth Venture and help others reach their goals with my Weekend Wealth Plan.

You can increase your income by turning more prospects into profitable customers. You can motivate employees and other business contacts to help you build profits. You can motivate bankers to offer you the cash you need. You can control others with the Power of Motivation.

You are clearly on your way to the success you deserve as a powerful Weekend Wealth Builder.

ENERGIZING YOUR WEEKEND WEALTH PLAN

You can multiply your profits with the help of others by applying the Power of Motivation successfully. You can turn on this power today by doing these things:

1. See how others are using the Power of Motivation on you right now—advertisers, salespeople, leaders. Find six examples in your daily life and analyze them.

2. Put the Power of Motivation to work for you. Use my four-step plan for applying this power on a test case: a supplier, a customer, an employee, an influential person. Watch them work hard for you.

3. Discover your customer's Buyer Buttons. What turns them on to buy from you? How can you use Buyer Buttons to increase your income and profits?

4. Use the Power of Motivation on others who can help you build your business profits. Discover and develop their motivation, reward them, then reinforce their action with appreciation. Use the power to get your way with others.

10

How Weekend Wealth Builders Multiply Profits With Smart Management Strategy

Every dollar has hidden profits—for the smart Weekend Wealth Builder.

These profits can spell the difference between an average enterprise and a highly profitable business venture. They can mean the difference between long years of struggle and short weeks to success.

The smart Weekend Wealth Builder has developed the techniques that spell the difference between success and failure. He has learned that his time and resources are very valuable—and that he should spend them as he spends his money: wisely and profitably. He has discovered that the difference between the almost-successful and the highly-successful is often the application of easily-learned techniques.

The smart Weekend Wealth Builder has discovered the Smart Management Strategies that can take anyone to the successful world of part-time profits.

TURNING SMART MANAGEMENT STRATEGY INTO INCREASED WEEKEND WEALTH

Once you've started your profitable Weekend Wealth Venture—as you have now—there are dozens of things you can do to increase your profits and reduce the time you spend with your enterprise.

You can multiply your successes by developing your own Success Priorities. You can learn how to increase profits with Creative Time. You can use Profit Planning to reach your goals. You can set and carry out your own Success Priorities and delegate Success Priorities to others in your enterprise.

You can also increase your venture profits by cutting losses through a simple Waste Audit. You can call in consultants at little or no cost to help you increase profitability. You can learn how major businesses build extra profits through standardization. And you can recycle wastes to get every available profit dollar from your successful Weekend Wealth Venture.

These are the successful steps you can follow to multiply your venture profits while cutting costs of your part-time opportunity. These are the advanced techniques used by the most successful Weekend Wealth Builders to multiply profits while they enjoy increased satisfaction from their venture. These are the trade secrets that hundreds of smart Weekend Wealth Builders would like to pass on to you.

MAKING MONEY WITH CREATIVE TIME

If there's one common activity that all highly successful Weekend Wealth Builders use, it's Creative Time. Most tell me that Creative Time is often the most profitable part of their enterprise.

Creative Time is time set aside for a creative Weekend Wealth Builder to use the powers of his conscious and subconscious mind on problems he faces. It's a time when problems are solved, when questions are answered, and when solutions are discovered. Creative Time can be the key to future success and profits.

Here's how you can use Creative Time to build your enterprise toward greater profitability:

* *Set aside Creative Time.* Plan a few minutes each day or each week for solving your venture problems through your mind powers.
* *Build your powers.* When Creative Time comes, relax in a quiet place and clear your mind of other thoughts and ideas. Prepare yourself for the reception of new solutions and improved methods.
* *Turn your mind on.* Now concentrate on the question you want answered or the problem you'd like solved. Explain it to an imaginary counselor. Rephrase the problem.
* *Write down possible solutions.* As they come to you, jot down answers to your question—no matter how unlikely. Your mind is working on the solution.
* *Follow up.* When Creative Time is over, compare some of the solutions you wrote down, mix them up together to come up with new solutions. Check out necessary facts.
* *Put solutions to work.* Try out one or more of the best solutions to your problem. Then take your improved situation back through the Creative Time process again to double-check it. Make sure it's the best solution for your problem or goal.

Many successful Weekend Wealth Builders feel that Creative Time is one of their greatest business assets. They set aside a half-hour or more each week for Creative Time. One venture builder, Lester S. of Billings, Montana, feels that his one hour a week of Creative Time is more productive than a full day's efforts by a full-time executive. Using Creative Time, Les has increased his income as a puppeteer to as much as $600 a month working on Saturdays only. Les uses his own creative powers to build his part-time venture into a satisfying—and rewarding—enterprise. You can, too.

HOW SMART WEEKEND WEALTH BUILDERS PLAN FOR FUTURE PROFITS

How would you like to decide today how much money you'll make with your venture next month, next year and three years from now? You can—with my Weekend Wealth Plan. You can come up with a realistic profit figure and count on it just as faithfully as you count on a check from your regular job. Here's how:

* Review your venture goals
* Break your goals into steps
* Plan your attack
* Activate your plan
* Spend your profits

Let's see how one particularly successful Weekend Wealth Builder planned for future profits—and succeeded.

Sherm D. Wrote His Own Check For The Future—And Cashed It

Sherm D. of Richmond, Virginia, had a dream for nearly 20 years. His dream was to make a living as a writer. He had only a high school education, but Sherm was determined to reach his goal.

Then one day Sherm realized that he really had no firm goal. Sure, he wanted to be a writer, but he had never decided how much money he was going to earn from writing, how he would built his part-time career, or what steps he should take to reach his goal. Sherm had made a few sales to smaller magazines but he had never planned for future profits. Here's what he finally did about it.

Sherm reviewed his venture goals—and decided to develop some new and more defined goals. Sherm decided that his time as a writer should be worth 20 dollars an hour. He promised himself that he would earn 10 dollars an hour part-time for the next six months, then 15 dollars an hour for the following six months—reaching his goal of 20 dollars an hour as a freelance article writer in one year. Sherm had reviewed his venture goals and broken his goals into easy steps.

Next, Sherm planned his attack. To earn ten dollars an hour, he would have to discover how much he could produce in an hour, how long it took to write and sell an average article, and the best places to sell these articles. His interest in camping brought to mind four magazines that he regularly subscribed to. Checking *Writer's Market*, he found that many of them paid about the same—200 dollars for a 2,000 word article or about 10 cents a word. At 10 dollars an hour, Sherm could spend a full 20 hours writing an article and still reach his goal.

Sherm now activated his plan and wrote to each of the editors with different ideas for articles. Two of them wrote back with assignments and Sherm was on his way. He quickly improved his productivity and, well before his deadline, Sherm was earning 20 dollars an hour as a freelance writer.

Why? Not because of increased talents. Sherm was the same person who had sold only a few articles in many years of trying. The difference was Profit Planning. Sherm was now planning future profits and developing those plans into realities. Sherm is a smart Weekend Wealth Builder. Actually he's now a smart *full-time* freelance article writer.

MULTIPLYING PROFITS WITH SUCCESS PRIORITIES

Many otherwise smart Weekend Wealth Builders miss success by inches because they don't use this simple technique: act by Success Priorities. A Success Priority is the rating of venture activities by their importance to your success and your goals. That is, you do the job that's most important to your success first, then the next most important and so on.

Here's how you can increase venture profits while you cut out wasted time by planning your activities by Success Priorities:

* List your venture activities
* Which activity is most important to your success?
* Which is the next most important activity?
* Now work on Activity #1 until it is completed
* Start on Activity #2, and so on

See how it works? Success Priorities are used by both big corporation executives and smart Weekend Wealth Builders.

How Frank E. Turned Success Priorities Into Easy Cash

Three evenings a week, Frank E. of Burlington, Vermont, operates a highly successful reupholstery business from his garage. Frank specializes in reupholstering restaurant booths and earns an impressive part-time salary for his efforts.

Frank's Weekend Wealth Venture hasn't always been this successful. In fact, a couple of years ago Frank was ready to quit—he just wasn't making enough money with his venture. Then he learned how to work by Success Priorities and it turned his profit picture around. Here's how he did it.

During his Creative Time, Frank discovered that he was wasting a lot of time in his venture. He built racks for his materials; he spent time cleaning up his shop and waiting for an order to come in. Frank woke up and decided that he was on the wrong road to his goal. He reviewed his goal of earning at least $500 a month in extra cash with his venture. He still wanted to reach that goal. He then listed all of the activities that are a part of reaching his goal:

* Gathering supplies
* Contacting restaurants about reupholstery
* Reupholstering booths

* Picking up and delivering booths
* Studying books and magazines on upholstery
* Promoting the business

Then Frank put them in the order of their importance to his goal:

* Contacting restaurants about reupholstery
* Promoting the business
* Picking up and delivering booths
* Reupholstering booths
* Gathering supplies
* Studying books and magazines on upholstery

Finally, Frank started on Activity#1—contacting restaurants about upholstery. He spent one of his days off each week talking with restaurant owners about his service and making bids on reupholstery jobs. At the same time, Frank contacted a local weekly newspaper about his business and was able to get a small feature about his unique venture in the paper—Activity #2. Once he had a few orders, Frank started on Activity #3—and so on. Frank was now working by Success Priorities. He did the most important thing to his Weekend Wealth goal first, then the next most important task, and then the next until he reached his goal.

Frank has more than reached his goal of earning an extra $500 a month with his part-time venture. He has also upgraded his regular job. With the experience from his part-time venture, Frank was able to get a full-time job as an upholsterer in a sofa factory at nearly twice the salary of his old job with a janitorial firm. Frank used his venture to increase his income in two ways—as a smart Weekend Wealth Builder.

EARNING BIGGER PROFITS BY DELEGATING SUCCESS PRIORITIES

The extra earning power that comes with activating your Success Priorities can be multiplied by setting up similar priorities for others who affect your venture. That is, you can help employees, suppliers, agents and customers work harder for you if you show them how your mutual Success Priorities can be built together.

Doris A. and Jacky L. operated a bulletin board service together. They supplied bulletin boards in stores and shopping centers where customers could post their ads for buying and selling personal items. There was no charge to the store. However, Doris and Jacky sold space on the top and bottom of the bulletin boards to local businessmen who wanted to advertise their full-time ventures.

By mutual agreement, Doris was the administrator/ad salesperson and Jacky was the worker/board poster. After six months, Doris could see that Jacky was losing interest in the venture and thought it less important than other things she wanted to do—even though the enterprise gave them both an ever-increasing income for a few hours' work.

One day, Doris and Jacky had coffee and talked about the problem. Jacky admitted that she was losing interest so they took time to review their goals, list the required activities and rate them as Success Priorities. Finally, each partner was delegated two or more of the activities and they talked about how these activities would help them reach their new goal: to build the business for one more year, then sell it and split the profits.

It worked. With renewed interest, Doris and Jacky turned to their venture with increased interest and the year quickly passed. They soon found a ready buyer for the part-time enterprise and they split the profit of more then $8 thousand.

Doris and Jacky got back on the right road to success by delegating Success Priorities.

RETRIEVING LOST PROFITS WITH A WASTE AUDIT

No matter how big or small your Weekend Wealth Venture has become, there are dozens of places where profits can be lost or overlooked—places that the smart Weekend Wealth Builder searches for.

A *Waste Audit* is simply a systematic search through your part-time enterprise for unused assets, lost profits and costly expenses. You can start your own Waste Audit right now and pull every potential profit dollar from your venture by doing these things:

* *Start a notebook.* Head it "Waste Audit" and begin writing down things that could be robbing you of potential profits: unused equipment that could be sold, wasted supplies, unsold time or products that could be wholesaled, overhead that could be reduced.

* *Write down remedies.* Use your Creative Time to think about remedies for each of your Waste Audit points. Wasted supplies: keep a better inventory, sell unused supplies, find a profitable use for scraps and unused supplies, etc.

* *Activate solutions.* Choose the best remedy for each point of waste and put it into action.

How Miles R. Increased Cash In His Pocket With A Waste Audit

Miles R.'s Waste Audit showed him he was wasting the most important commodity of all: time. Miles made wall plaques with advertisements from old newspapers decoupaged onto them. He decided to streamline production and cut the time it took to produce each plaque.

First, Miles discovered it was becoming too expensive to seek out and purchase old newspapers just for the ads in them. He decided to choose the best ads he'd seen and have them reprinted on old-looking newsprint, then hand-tear them to look authentic.

Next, Miles decided that brushing on the varnish on each plaque was too time-consuming. His supplier told him about sprayers and even sold him one on credit to get him started. Miles cut the time needed to finish a plaque by more than half.

Finally, Miles talked with area gift shops until he found an energetic sales representative who called on most of them with gift merchandise. He then contacted the agent and asked him to represent his line of "old ad" plaques. He would—for a percentage—and Miles soon had twice as many orders as before. Best of all, Miles used his Waste Audit to cut production time in half so he was spending no more time and earning a much greater profit with his rebuilt Weekend Wealth Venture.

HOW TO MOTIVATE OTHERS TO HELP WITH YOUR WASTE AUDIT

You can improve your profit picture by getting others to help you cut costs and improve productivity. You can cut costs and improve productivity. You can cut expenses and increase income with suggestions and Waste Audits from these people:

* Employees - Ask them to suggest methods of increasing profits in their segment of your enterprise.
* Friends and relatives - Get a fresh eye to look over your venture for possible losses from wasted assets.
* Hire no-cost consultants - Many areas have organizations for retired citizens who have business experience and can volunteer a few hours to assist small businesses with their problems. You can often gain nearly a half-century of practical advice and experience through these volunteers. Ask your chamber of commerce.
* Check your telephone book - You may find a small business consultant in your area who can earn you many times his hourly fee with practical advice on how to cut waste and improve profits in your opportunity.
* Discover new ideas in books - Just as you found dozens of new and profitable ideas in this book you can find it in others. My book, *How to Earn Over $50,000 a Year at Home*, offers many unique techniques that you can profit from. Other opportunity books are available from the same publisher, Parker Publishing Company, Inc., West Nyack. N.Y. 10994.

Any one of these sources can be worth hundreds or even thousands of dollars to you in extra profits. Try them. Many other people are interested in seeing you succeed with your Weekend Wealth Venture.

STANDARDIZING PROFITS IN YOUR WEEKEND WEALTH VENTURE

Once your part-time venture is on the road to profits, you'll discover that many of the things you do will be repeated. If you're making a product, you'll go through the same steps each time to put it together. If you're selling a service to others, you will be asking the same questions of your clients and talking with them about the same things.

Smart Weekend Wealth Builders use this repetition of activity for their own profit—they *standardize* their activities to make their venture more profitable and less time-consuming. Here's how:

Smart Weekend Wealth Builders standardize—

    Procedure

    Production

    Sources

    Communications

The best example of this technique that I can think of is the story of Ray B. of Albuquerque, New Mexico. Roy was an exporter of beautiful Indian turquoise jewelry from the southwest.

Roy standardized his venture procedure by clearly defining the object and methods of his enterprise—then making sure it was carried through his entire venture. He made a chart for the wall above his desk that showed how and where orders came in, how they should be processed and followed up, and how they should be paid for—cash with order or thirty-day account depending on the customer.

Then Roy actually standardized production or the processing of an order. The order was written on his own special form, passed on to his wife who packaged the order and checked off each item, then shipped it by pre-decided methods depending on weight and destination. The order was then reviewed by Roy before shipment to make sure it was complete and exactly as the customer requested it. The paperwork was then filed for future reference.

Sources were also standardized. Roy had three different sources for his turquoise jewelry. Two were in New Mexico and one was in neighboring Arizona. The largest source specialized in necklaces and earrings, another made rings and a third made special jewelry to order. Roy kept the most popular items in stock and special-ordered others as needed.

Finally, Roy standardized communications with his customers. He developed a form that was like a friendly letter yet allowed Roy to check appropriate boxes and tell the customer what he had ordered, when he could expect to receive it and how payment was to be made. He also printed up packing slips that went with the order. Roy even developed a special list of standard comments, numbered them and saved time for his wife when she typed letters. He would request a "letter to Mr. Smith with paragraphs 7, 2, 9A and 4, inserting October 1 as the delivery date." His wife had a copy of the sample paragraphs and could quickly type up the letter—saving time and money for both.

Roy knows he made thousands of extra dollars with his standardization of procedure, production, sources and communications. You can, too.

RECYCLING MONEY BACK INTO YOUR OWN POCKET

You've probably heard it said that it's the pennies that make the dollars. It's especially true in business. In a huge business that works on a small profit margin—like a grocery store that earns a three percent profit on its gross income—a few extra cents on each profit dollar can quickly multiply profits.

It's the same in a small business venture—except that you actually have more control on your profits than does the owner of a huge grocery store. You can increase profits easier than a larger business can—by recycling waste. Ask yourself:

* What byproducts does my venture produce?

* How could I reuse them?
* How could others reuse them?
* Is there a special need somewhere for them?
* How could I quickly turn them into cash?

How Leslie H. Turned Waste Into Extra Profits

Leslie H. of Sacramento, California, operated a successful part-time doll fashion venture before discovering a profitable use for scraps. For two years, Leslie made miniature fashions and sold them through specialty shops throughout California. Meanwhile, scrap fabric began piling up in boxes in the corner of her garage-workshop.

One day, a neighbor stopped by for coffee and asked about the boxes. Leslie told her what they were and said she'd sure like to find a use for them. The friend suggested that she make her own rag dolls and stuff them with the scraps. Great idea.

With the assistance of her helpful neighbor, Leslie makes and sells an extra $100 to $200 a month worth of rag dolls—plus, she's found a method of recycling waste from her doll clothing production. Since then, Leslie's also decided to make and sell miniature quilts from the scraps. She markets both the quilts and dolls through her regular buyers. Leslie is a smart Weekend Wealth Builder.

HOW OTHER WEEKEND WEALTH BUILDERS WORK BY PRIORITY AND CUT WASTE

The profitable techniques for increasing profits through Success Priorities and Waste Audits are as many and varied as the number of smart Weekend Wealth Builders. Here are two more who may give you an idea you can use profitably:

* Marv I. operates a unique Weekend Wealth Venture in Boulder, Colorado—a weekend pet-sitter service. Marv takes special care of pets for those who are going out of town for a few days. Marv was able to recycle many ideas and increase profits substantially by discovering a couple in Denver who oper-

ated a similar service and trading techniques and ideas. Marv eliminated wasted advertising dollars, was able to increase fees to meet his competition's, and discovered a new way to attract customers economically. Marv learned how to recycle ideas from others.

* Sandra L. runs a newspaper clipping service in Chicago. Many businesses and important people would like to have copies of newspaper stories that appear about them. Sandra made a handsome part-time profit cutting out stories about clients in local papers. She also cut waste by (1) keeping track of the most used newspapers and dropping others that had nothing about her clients, and (2) contacting smaller businessmen who advertised in metropolitan papers and offering to send them copies of their ads for a small monthly fee. Sandra knows how to earn extra profits by cutting waste and finding uses for scraps from her enterprise.

YOU CAN MULTIPLY VENTURE PROFITS WITH SMART MANAGEMENT STRATEGY

You can find the hidden profit in every dollar with the Weekend Wealth Plan.

You can enjoy extra profits from your Weekend Wealth Venture by developing your own Success Priorities, using Creative Time wisely, and reaching your financial goals with Profit Planning.

You can cut waste in your venture with a simple Waste Audit. You can use the time and talents of small business consultants—often free of charge. You now know how to standardize your venture and even recycle wastes in your business to squeeze every dollar for the most profit.

In this chapter, you've seen how people much like yourself—from all parts of the country—have used the simple Weekend Wealth Plan to increase their income and their satisfaction with Smart Management Strategy. You've joined the smart Weekend Wealth Builders.

ENERGIZING YOUR WEEKEND WEALTH PLAN

Discover the extra dollars of pure profit in every venture dollar. Use Smart Management Strategy to eliminate waste and work by priority. Do these things today:

1. Start using Creative Time to build your venture. Set aside a special time and place to use your creative mind powers for the problems that face your venture. Discover new solutions to old problems. Find new ways to operate your venture efficiently and successfully.

2. Use Profit Planning to build future income. Review your venture goals, break them into steps, activate your plan and turn the future into a growing reflection of today. Use your powers for profit.

3. Review your Weekend Wealth Venture for Success Priorities. Use your greatest asset—your time—wisely and effectively by completing tasks in the order of their importance to your ultimate goal. Turn your time into cash with Success Priorities.

4. Delegate your venture's Success Priorities to others who are assisting you with your venture. Show them how they will benefit from the completion of your venture's goals.

5. Establish your own Waste Audit. Cut losses throughout your venture by systematically searching your enterprise for ways to cut expenses and increase income through recycling.

6. Standardize your operation for greater profits. Set up your own system for venture procedure, production, sources and communications.

7. Recycle profit dollars by turning scraps and extra time from your enterprise into more dollars. Use the Weekend Wealth Plan to find new uses for waste.

11

Unlock The Vault
To Hidden Profits
In Your Weekend
Wealth Venture

The smart Weekend Wealth Builder soon finds himself with a major problem—*too much money.*

His income quickly rises and he soon enjoys the added luxuries that spare time income can bring. The problem is that he may not know how to keep the flow coming. His income is more than his expenses, but he's not sure how to keep this ratio when costs rise or income hits a seasonal slump.

He also has to face a growing expense: taxes. As he earns more profits, his partner in business—Uncle Sam—requires more. The smart business builder knows he can't underpay his partner—but he sure doesn't want to overpay him either.

The solution, again, is the Weekend Wealth Plan. This proven plan for part-time venture success can show you how to both keep the profit flow coming and keep your already rich Uncle from taking your profits.

KEEPING YOUR VENTURE PROSPEROUS
THE EASY WAY

If you're like the average Weekend Wealth Builder you're not too crazy about keeping detailed records of everything you do. You don't care for adding up long columns of figures and trying to make budgets and books balance.

You *do* like to count money, though. You enjoy the satisfaction of discovering how much of every income dollar goes into your own pocket. You love to project into the future and see your profits rise higher and higher. You want to outsmart Uncle Sam at his own game and take advantage of all the tax loopholes you can with your venture.

I'm going to show you a simple system for keeping records that will make it easy and enjoyable for you to see just how much you're making with your enterprise—plus how to keep Uncle Sam from taking more than he really needs to take for taxes. You'll soon learn:

* The Weekend Wealth Simple Record System
* How to quickly tabulate current profits
* How to keep a simple inventory and know what you have at all times
* How to use your records to insure you get the loan you want from any bank
* How to estimate the profit on every unit you make or every hour you sell
* How to insure profits on every transaction

* How to reduce taxes through completely legal tax loopholes and business secrets

Sound exciting? It is. This chapter offers the key to a new horizon. Even if you *hate* math and keeping records you'll enjoy the challenge of starting your own profitable record system that will both make you money and save you money without a lot of wasted time.

THE WEEKEND WEALTH SIMPLE RECORD SYSTEM

There are many ways to keep a record of your Weekend Wealth Venture's income and expenses. You can throw receipts in a drawer and, at the end of the year, hand them to an accountant. You can keep intricate books to tell you exactly where every last penny went, to whom and why. Or you can have the best of both worlds—simplicity and thoroughness—with my Weekend Wealth Simple Record System. Here's how it works:

There are five sources and uses for money in your Weekend Wealth Venture:

* Assets - Things you own
* Liabilities - Money you owe
* Capital - The difference or what your venture is worth
* Income - Money earned in exchange for your product or service
* Expenses - Money paid to produce and sell your product or service

How Milt D. Set Up His Efficient Record System In Minutes

Milt D. of Minneapolis, Minnesota, operates a successful paperback book exchange on weekends and sells his used books at area flea marts. Within a few months from its inception, Milt's business venture was bringing him an extra 100 to 200 dollars a weekend. The problem was that he didn't keep good enough records to know where the money was coming from or going to.

Here's how Milt set up his books in minutes. He purchased a notebook with dividers and had a section for each of his cash sources and uses.

Assets	- Retail value of paperbacks on hand Estimated value of display table, chair and cash box
Liabilities	- Books held but not paid for yet - Equipment not paid for yet
Capital	- The difference between assets and liabilities—known as net worth
Income	- Money earned from selling paperbacks (totaled at the end of each day)
Expenses	- Cost of purchasing books - Cost of purchasing equipment

Each time that Milt would receive money or pay money out he would note it on the appropriate page of his notebook. For a small business, this type of record system is highly practical and efficient, and is used by many successful Weekend Wealth Builders.

TURNING A CASH JOURNAL INTO CASH

Rather than have a separate page for each type of entry, many smart venture builders use what's called a *Cash Journal* to keep track of all incoming and outgoing cash in their enterprise. Larger full-time businesses often use a "double entry bookkeeping system" but most part-time business builders don't have the time to mess with complicated bookkeeping and accounting systems. Most prefer a simple Cash Journal that has lines for each time money is spend or received, who it came from or where it went to, and a column for each of the things it may have gone for.

Keith K. purchased a simple ten-column journal at a stationery store and, after heading the description columns with "date" and "Paid To/Received From" he headed his ten columns like this for his lawnmower repair service:

Income   - Repair service
               - Parts sales
               - Lawnmower rental
Expenses   - Cost of parts
               - Labor
               - Shop rental
               - Utilities
               - Taxes (Sales and Income)
               - Insurance
               - Miscellaneous

Since Keith operated his lawnmower repair service out of his own garage he decided to charge himself a reasonable rent and legally deducted a percentage of his mortgage payment as a business expense. Keith also paid himself ten dollars an hour for labor in his shop.

The greatest advantage to the Cash Journal is that it offers a simple method of keeping track of all incoming and outgoing money. Weekly bank deposits are broken down into categories so you know exactly where your income came from. You may discover that one aspect of your venture is more profitable than another. You may want to drop one or two products in your line—or you may discover that the income on a certain day is too small to justify your working that day.

Your Cash Journal can also tell you if you're paying too much for raw materials in relation to the amount of income you earn with them. In Keith's lawnmower repair service, his "Income - Parts sales" must be greater than his "Expenses - Cost of Parts"; otherwise, he's losing money. Your Cash Journal will help you keep track of these profit ratios quickly and easily.

DISCOVERING YOUR WORTH WITH LEDGERS

You can keep track of your other categories of value—your assets, liabilities and capital or net worth—

with ledgers. A *Ledger* is simply a card or piece of paper that keeps track of certain figures for you. There are basically three types of ledgers in the Weekend Wealth Simple Record System:

* *Assets Ledger* - There's a card for each type of asset: equipment, cash on hand, money owed to you but not collected yet (accounts receivable), and merchandise on hand but not sold.

* *Liabilities Ledger* - To keep track of money you owe to others, you need a card for each type of liability: equipment payments, supplies not paid for, taxes due. These are often called "accounts payable."

* *Capital Ledger* - This ledger usually only has one card, the "capital" card. On it you can keep track of your starting capital, any additions of capital you've since made, and "capital draws" or money you've taken from your venture for personal use.

Not all small weekend ventures need ledgers, but if your venture uses and issues credit, has a lot of equipment or a number of other assets, you may want to set up ledgers to keep better control on the value of your venture.

How Rich A. Uncomplicated His Venture With Ledgers

Rich A. would sometimes forget what he had on hand—and lose a sale. Rich operates a small antique shop evenings and weekends from his home in Winnemucca, Nevada. He owns some of the antiques in his house-shop, but most of them are sold on consignment for others. The problem was that he had so many antiques spread throughout his large older home that he sometimes missed a sale because he either didn't remember or couldn't find a piece that someone was looking for.

Then Rich decided to take the advice of a business consultant and set up a Ledger system. It was actually a combined Ledger-Inventory because each piece on hand had a card that showed the original purchase price, the owner of the piece, its age and value, and its location within his large house-shop. He could quickly find any piece in his home.

Rich also had an "Accounts Receivable" Ledger for customers who were purchasing antiques from him either on credit or lay-away. These accounts were valuable assets to his business. Rich knew that he could take these "IOUs" to the bank and get a loan against them if he wanted to.

Rich increased his income and kept better track of his valuable assets with a simple Ledger system. So can you.

INCREASING PROFITS WITH INVENTORY RECORDS

You can set up a simple inventory system that will bring you extra profit dollars and help you reduce waste. The Weekend Wealth Simple Record System offers you a method of keeping track of your inventory in minutes if you are selling or manufacturing a product for others. Depending on your own venture's needs you can use some or all of this valuable inventory system.

If you manufacture your own product you can have three simple records—on cards or sheets as best fit your venture:

* Raw materials
* Materials in progress
* Finished Products

If you are a middleman and sell a product that is produced by another Weekend Wealth Builder or entrepreneur, you can keep track of your inventory with cards filed:

* By item
* By type
* By supplier
* By value
* By date received

A good example of a smart Weekend Wealth Builder's inventory system is one set up by Al V. of Tampa, Florida. Al operates a highly successful craft business. Al makes and sells his own decorative lamps and also stocks crafts from other venture builders. Al's shop is set up in his garage and his wife, Del, sells crafts from the shop-garage while Al is at his regular job driving-long-haul truck.

Al set up an inventory card system for his manufacturing business. When listing raw materials for lamps—wood, electric cords and sockets, varnish, shades, metal accessories—Al would write them into a section of his inventory book called "Raw Materials." Once he started working with the materials to form a lamp Al wrote them off the "Raw Materials" section and into "Materials In Progress." Finally, when the lamps were completed, Al marked them out of that book and wrote the number and model of the lamps he had made in the section marked "Finished Products."

Why? Because Al could then easily tell customers whether he had a certain lamp in stock, how long it would be before he would have it, what the value of his raw materials or completed lamps was, which lamps were moving the fastest, and what quantity of raw materials he needed to order. Al's inventory system took only a few minutes a day but it made him many hundreds of dollars in extra profits and quick sales.

Al's inventory of other craft items sold in his shop was different. Each item had a small 3×5 card that showed the owner's name, the item description, the price, the date of receipt and other information that would help him sell the product. Al filed these cards by type of craft, but he could have just as easily filed them by the supplier or consignor, by price range, by item or by any other method.

Al found hidden profits in his Weekend Wealth Venture by keeping simple records of his inventory of merchandise.

SUMMING UP SUCCESS WITH
YOUR PROFIT AND LOSS STATEMENT

Many smart Weekend Wealth Builders find extra motivation in knowing just how profitable their venture is. They can quickly discover just how much they're making with their enterprise and compare it with the number of hours put in or the amount of cash invested. They make this discovery with a simple *Profit and Loss Statement.*

A Profit and Loss Statement is used by even the biggest

businesses in the nation to discover whether their enterprise is profitable and decide how to improve their operation effectively.

A Profit and Loss Statement tells the venture owner, his bankers and backers, and anyone else he share it with:

* *Income* - How much income was earned and where it came from
* *Expenses* - What it cost to earn this income and what the money went for.

Here's a typical Profit and Loss Statement for a small part time business called *Model Railroading News*, a monthly publication for model railroaders:

INCOME:

Subscriptions (1400 @ $9 each)	$ 12,600	
Advertising (Classified/Display)	$ 8,250	
Interest received on bank account	$ 525	
Total income		$21,375

EXPENSES:

Printing and Typesetting	$ 8,103	
Postage and Permits	$ 1,320	
Addressing	$ 336	
Rent	$ 1,200	
Utilities and Telephone	$ 572	
Advertising and Publicity	$ 4,128	
Miscellaneous	$ 791	
Total expenses		$16,450

NET PROFIT (Before Taxes) | | $ 4,925 |

From this Profit and Loss Statement, owner Ann T. discovered that about 23 percent of her income was profit. She also found out that about 59 percent of her income came from subscriptions and another 39 percent from advertising. Talking with other publishers, Ann learned that her percentage of income from advertising should actually be more than that from subscriptions—she would work to improve this total. Ann also saw that her major expense—Printing and Typesetting—took up a full 38 percent of her budget. She promised herself to check into alternative publishing sources and methods. She could purchase some typesetting equipment and do part of the work herself. She could ask for bids and take the lowest. She could trade some of her printing bill for advertising.

Ann's Profit and Loss Statement helped her build her venture not only by building motivation, but also by showing her where she could increase income and lower expenses. A P & L Statement can do the same for your enterprise.

INCREASING PROFITS WITH COST CONTROL

Here's another valuable use for your Weekend Wealth Simple Record System—*Cost Control.* Cost Control is simply shaving your costs of operation down to the bare minimum while still producing or selling the highest quality product or service.

Here's how Cost Control works:

* Estimate costs per unit or per hour
* Control both ends
* Improve costs (and profits)

Let's watch Cost Control in action with a successful Weekend Wealth Builder.

How George W. Collected Bigger Profits With Cost Control

George W. operates a successful flower stand in a Los Angeles suburb. On weekends he purchases flowers from wholesalers and breaks them into bundles to sell to visitors at cemeteries in the San Fernando Valley.

To operate profitably, George decided to put Cost Control into action. First he estimated costs per unit. He sold packages of six flowers and a dozen flowers at five and ten dollars. The flowers (a mixture that varied depending on wholesale prices and the season) cost him two dollars a dozen. His overhead and supplies—wrapping paper, signs, ferns, truck and gasoline—added another fifty cents a dozen to the price for a total cost per dozen of $2.50—a mark up of 400 percent.

The next step in Cost Control for George was to "control both ends." That is, George wanted to make sure that he could purchase flowers at this price and sell enough of them to insure a profit through volume. He controlled his wholesale costs by mixing the flowers he purchased to average two dollars a dozen. He bought some at one dollar, some at three dollars and even some at four dollars a dozen—but he mixed his packages so that they cost the same year round. George controlled his flow of customers by studying the amount of business he did at each of the cemeteries for one weekend, then he chose the most profitable one as his regular stand. He then built up business by repeat customers who came in often.

Finally, George used Cost Control to improve profits. He shopped for wholesale florists who could give him a better price or give him free ferns with his purchase. He improved profits by closing up early and selling his remaining flowers door-to-door in nearby neighborhoods. He increased profits through encouraging customers to take special "remembrance bouquets" home with them and even sold them vases.

George now works three days a week at his flower stand and spends the other four days enjoying life because he used the techniques of Cost Control to turn a Weekend Wealth Venture into a full-time business.

HOW TO LEGALLY AVOID PAYING TAXES ON YOUR WEEKEND WEALTH VENTURE

How would you like to reduce or completely eliminate paying taxes on profits from your part-time enterprise? You can—with completely legal methods used by hundreds of smart Weekend Wealth Builders across the country.

Uncle Sam is your partner in business. Under our capitalistic system, the government sets up and watches over the economic system that allows all of us to take advantage of opportunities for profits and lets us earn extra money according to what we produce for others. As our silent partner, Uncle Sam takes his salary in the form of taxes—a percentage of your income after certain allowable deductions. The key to saving money on your taxes is knowing and using as many allowable tax deductions as possible.

Here are some of the taxes that your partner, Uncle Sam, is paid:

Federal Taxes	- Income taxes
	- Social Security taxes
	- Excise tax
	- Unemployment tax
State Taxes	- Income taxes
	- Sales taxes
	- Franchise taxes
	- Unemployment taxes
Local Taxes	- Personal property taxes
	- Real estate taxes
	- Sales taxes
	- Business licenses and taxes

Uncle Sam, in this case, represents all governments from the nation's capital to your local city hall. Each must be paid a percentage of your profits. As a smart Weekend Wealth Builder you can reduce or even completely eliminate many of the taxes that are heaped upon the enterprising. You can take advantage of so-called "loopholes" in the tax laws and use the money you save to build your business and enjoy life more.

TAX LOOPHOLES YOU CAN PROFIT FROM NOW

To encourage growth and development in certain areas of businesses, the governments got together to allow the smart businessman to reduce his tax obligation by doing certain things. Some of these tax loopholes are only for the speculative investor, but many can be used even by the smallest businessman to reduce or eliminate his tax bill.

Here are six ways you can minimize your taxes legally as a smart Weekend Wealth Builder:

Interest paid - *You can completely deduct, as a legal expense, any interest paid on a business debt.*

Dick D. operates a parking lot cleaning service. His sweeper machine is being purchased on time with payments of $107.20 a month. Of that amount, $62.45 goes for interest on the loan and is a completely tax deductible expense.

Depreciation - *As they are used by a business, buildings and equipment wear out and are less valuable to their owners. The government gives the smart businessman the opportunity to deduct this estimated loss as depreciation and reduce his tax obligation accordingly.*

Linda S. has built a supplemental income in her spare time with a snow cone machine that she can easily load in the back of her station wagon. Linda purchased the machine for $900. With a life expectancy for the machine of about four years, Linda is allowed to depreciate or deduct one-quarter of its cost each year—$225.

Capital Gains - *Many of the assets or things of value in your business are Capital Assets. If you sell one of these assets and make money on it–a gain–you now have a Capital Gain. The profit you made on this sale is taxed at just half the rate it would be if you were to receive the same money as ordinary income. This applies to equipment, real estate and other assets that are not normally sold in the course of your business.*

Mike S. purchased a small piece of land near the edge of town from which he sold his fruits and vegetables. A couple of years later, the city had expanded and nearly reached his lot. It was worth more than double what he paid for it. In selling it, Mike received a profit of $7,200, but since it was a gain on a capital asset, he was taxed on the gain as if it were just half that amount—$3,600. The profit was greater than that of his fruit stand.

Taxes - *Taxes paid to your governmental business partner are tax deductible. That's right. If you paid $300 in business taxes last year you may deduct it from this year's tax return as a completely legal business expense.*

Phyllis W. operated her doll hospital out of a spare bedroom in her home. She was not only able to deduct the income and sales taxes she paid from her tax obligation, she was also allowed to deduct a percentage of her property taxes based on the portion of the home she used exclusively for her business venture.

Investment Credit - *Uncle Sam says that if you purchased a new or used depreciable property for use in your business you may qualify for an investment credit. Contact the Internal Revenue Service or your accountant to discover how much of a credit you can use.*

Harold T. operates a weekend cab service shuttling people from Las Vegas' airport to downtown hotels and casinos. Since about 50 percent of his mileage is business related and the other half is for personal use during the week, Harold earned one-half the tax credit for his investment. His cab cost $7,129. Half of that is $3,564.50. He earned a tax Investment Credit of 10 percent or $356.45.

Self-Employed Retirement Plans - *You may be entitled to a limited deduction for contributions to a retirement benefit plan for yourself as a partially self-employed person.*

Sam C. sells exotic herbs and spices through the mails. His part-time venture gives him an extra income of $6,000 to $7,000 a year—$750 of which he can put away in his own retirement fund to draw on when he's 65. Sam has six more years to go, but already he's adding up the money he'll have thanks to Uncle Sam and his Weekend Wealth Venture.

YOU CAN UNLOCK THE VAULT TO HIDDEN PROFITS WITH SIMPLE VENTURE RECORDS AND TAX LOOPHOLES

You can add hundreds of extra profit dollars to your income this year with the secrets and techniques offered in this chapter.

You can discover loose profit dollars with your own Weekend Wealth Simple Record System and unique methods of Cost Control that help you eliminate profit waste and use every available dollar in your business opportunity.

You can reduce or even eliminate your venture's tax bill by learning and using the many tax loopholes that legally cut your obligation to your partner in business, Uncle Sam.

You can enjoy the use of more of your profit dollars by applying the simple recordkeeping methods and practical tax credits used by thousands of smart Weekend Wealth Builders.

ENERGIZING YOUR WEEKEND WEALTH PLAN

Take advantage of our government's encouragement to growing businesses—set up your own simple record system and use available tax loopholes by doing these things:

1. Plan your own Weekend Wealth Simple Record System. Write down your own five sources and uses for money: assets, liabilities, capital, income and expenses.

2. Start your own Cash Journal to help you keep track of where your money comes from and where it goes. Make a column for each of your major areas of income and expenses and enter checks written, cash paid and received.

3. Set up your own Ledgers as needed by your enterprise—accounts payable, accounts receivable, inventory (raw materials, in progress, completed).

4. Make out your first Profit and Loss Statement to discover just how profitable your venture is. Analyze it for possible ways of increasing your profits.

5. Talk with your accountant or the Internal Revenue Service about legal tax loopholes that can help you in your Weekend Wealth Venture. Their help can save you hundreds—even thousands—of profit dollars.

Dynamic Pyramid Methods That Can Turn Weekend Wealth Builders Into Full-Time Fortune Builders

Money isn't everything—but it's sure a great way to keep score!

With money you can improve your lifestyle and add comfort and convenience to your days. You can enjoy a finer home, a sleeker car, a larger recreation vehicle. You can include many luxuries in your list of necessities.

With money you can have the security you desire. You can protect yourself from the high waves of life. You can stockpile money for a rainy day or a stormy week. You can purchase insurance against things that threaten your future.

With money you can feel the satisfaction of giving yourself and others what you want and deserve from life. You can see that your product or service is of real value to others. You can actually trade this value—money—for the things that will bring you satisfaction. You can find your spot in life and take greater advantage of each day with the power that money brings you as a Weekend Wealth Builder.

DEVELOPING YOUR WEEKEND WEALTH PLAN FOR FUTURE PROFITS

Now that you've seen my Weekend Wealth Plan take you from doubt and hesitation to confidence and extra cash, you're ready to consider the next alternative—turning your successful Weekend Wealth Venture into a Full-Time Fortune Builder.

In the coming pages of this final chapter you're going to see how other successful Weekend Wealth Builders have built a better tomorrow for themselves with Venture Expansion. You'll see the four dynamic steps to expansion; how to start your own Research and Development Department; how to make increased profits with venture experts and how to make your own contingency plan to insure your successful future.

You'll also learn how the smartest of the Weekend Wealth Builders use the secrets of diversification to build their spare time enterprises into full-time moneymakers. You'll join the ranks of the entrepreneur, then see how to start new ventures and buy up old ones profitably. Finally, you'll discover how the successful business builder puts his cash to work for even greater profits with less work.

Let's get going!

FOUR DYNAMIC STEPS TO VENTURE EXPANSION

Once you have discovered and built up your own successful Weekend Wealth Venture, you can use your knowledge—plus the techniques of successful venture builders—to expand your enterprise into a Full-Time Fortune Builder with these four simple steps:

* *Operate your Weekend Wealth Venture profitably.* Make sure that your enterprise is running efficiently and profitably before you start to expand.
* *Analyze the venture's successes and failures.* Discover how and why it has been a successful venture: strong Wealth-Building Blocks; Smart Management Strategy; Profit Accelerators; High Profit Power Tactics or other Weekend Wealth-Building Techniques.
* *Improve on a good thing.* Find at least three things you can do right now to make your venture even more profitable and efficient. Review earlier chapters and techniques in this book.
* *Build your Weekend Wealth Venture into a Full-Time Fortune Builder.* Start by finding new sources and markets for your product or service. Then sell your venture's benefits to these people. Finally, shift into high gear and multiply sales and profits.

How Fred M. Used Venture Expansion Techniques To Multiply His Income

Fred M. enjoyed working his Weekend Wealth Builder—raising guinea pigs and gerbils for pet shops—much more than he liked his full-time job at the tire factory. One day, he had had it and decided that he was going to expand his venture into a full-time enterprise and quit his regular job within six months. Here's how he did it.

First, Fred made sure that his enterprise was operating profitably. He made out a Profit and Loss Statement that showed he was making a hefty $12 to $18 an hour with his spare time venture.

Next, Fred analyzed the venture's successes and failures to discover how he could make his venture better. He discovered that he sold a high percentage of his rodents to three pet shops in the area that were members of a larger chain. He also discovered that one particular feed he was using made the rodents grow at a faster rate than other feeds.

Then, Fred put this knowledge to work for him. He contacted the main office of the pet shop chain and set up an appointment to talk with them. On a day off from his regular job, Fred sold the chain a contract for enough gerbils and guinea pigs over the next year to bring him a full-time profit. He also purchased a large quantity of the special feed at a big discount.

Finally, Fred took action by building his venture in his spare time until he couldn't afford *not* to quit his regular job. Fred was now in business for himself and his profits are still growing. Fred earns more than $30,000 a year with his Full-Time Fortune Builder—plus, he earns his own satisfaction.

WHY SMART WEEKEND WEALTH BUILDERS NEVER RUN OUT OF PROFITABLE IDEAS

I'd like to pass along to you what I feel is probably the greatest secret in the Weekend Wealth Plan. I can't really take credit for it, though. I've found it again and again in the lives of the most successful Weekend Wealth Builders I've studied. It's so simple I'm sure that you'll be able to put it into action the moment you hear about it.

Here it is:

> *Never withdraw from the principal–*
> *only from the interest.*

That is, once you've built your Weekend Wealth Venture and are enjoying its success, only use the *profits* from your venture to expand or build a new venture. That idea applies to both money and ideas. Not only should your expansion capital come from your original venture, but so should your ideas for greater ventures. You should be constantly reinvesting some of the profits from your successful

Weekend Wealth Venture into new ideas for profits. Here's how one smart venture builder put these ideas to work for him:

Hank C. operated a part-time recreation vehicle rental service in southern California. On his way to work at a furniture store, Hank would stop in shopping center parking lots and on residential streets to put a small handout under the wipers of recreation vehicles. It told the owners that he would help them pay for their RVs by renting them to others for a percentage of the rental fee. He had many prospects waiting.

Hank's income from this spare time venture was more than $150 a weekend—about $8,000 a year. Smart Hank decided to set aside *ten percent* of his profits in a special Research and Development Fund. With it he would look for better ways to make money in his spare time.

Then one day it struck him. He was driving through an exclusive residential area in Los Angeles and saw more than a dozen motorhomes and trailers parked at the side of the road. Writing on the sides of two large trucks proclaimed the reason: "Twentieth Century Fox." They were filming a movie and needed the RVs for dressing rooms. Hank stopped and talked with one of the location assistants. "Yeah, we always need portable dressing rooms on call." He told Hank whom to contact at the studio.

Within weeks Hank was operating a new division to his profitable RV rental service called "Location Homes." He rented RVs to the studios for use as dressing rooms, makeup rooms, location offices and even for use in the movies. The studios often used the units for months at a time—at a hefty rental fee. Hank was now earning a full-time income from his expanded Weekend Wealth Venture.

HIRING EXPERTS TO MULTIPLY YOUR PROFITS

Would you hire someone to help you expand your business if he could bring you two, three, five or ten times his salary? Sure you would. And so would other smart Weekend

Wealth Builders. That's why they often hire these experts to help them find additional profits in their venture:

* *Accountants* - A smart accountant can save you thousands of dollars each year in lower taxes and improved profits by showing you where you can take advantage of tax incentives and also reduce your ratio of expenses to income.

* *Attorneys* - Lawyers can not only get you out of legal trouble, they can keep you out of trouble. That's how smart Weekend Wealth Builders use them. They review contracts, organization plans, partnership a-greements, patent and franchise filings, covenants, and a dozen other agreements to make sure they conform to the law. They can often make or save you thousands of dollars in just one consultation hour.

* *Marketing experts* - Once you've built your venture in-to a full-time enterprise, you'll know that the most important step in the venture cycle is Marketing: getting your goods sold to the greatest number of customers. The Yellow Pages of a nearby metropoli-tan area will offer the names of many marketing ex-perts who can help you improve your marketing techniques and give you new profits.

* *Sales organizations* - To expand your venture to a full-time moneymaker, you may want to hire sales representatives who will sell your product or service to a wider field of customers. Since they work on a percentage of sales they will be anxious to make you more money. Contact sales reps and organizations through industry publications, sales magazines and through the Yellow Pages from different metropolitan areas (check with your library for out-of-state phone books).

The smartest Weekend Wealth Builder is not the one who tries to do everything himself, but the one who knows how to hire those who will make him more money than they cost. The businessperson with expansion on his mind will delegate some of his duties to those with specific knowledge—and profit from their efforts.

HOW SMART WEEKEND WEALTH BUILDERS
EVICT "FAILURE" FROM THEIR VOCABULARY

For most people the future is a question mark (?). They don't know what tomorrow will bring—and they're really not prepared to face it anyway.

For Weekend Wealth Builders the future is a big exclamation point (!). They don't know what tomorrow will bring either—but they have a pretty good idea and they've planned what they will do when it gets here. They're ready to succeed.

You can be, too, with the Weekend Wealth Plan. You can use tomorrow to increase your venture's size and profits. You can use tomorrow to reach your personal goals. You can use tomorrow to grasp the success you're searching for—if you're prepared for its arrival. Here's how the Weekend Wealth Builders take advantage of tomorrow before it arrives:

* *Discover possibilities* - Ask yourself: what could happen tomorrow, next month, next year that will have an affect on your venture? Positive? Negative?
* *Probability* - What are the chances that these things will occur? High? Low? Extremely low? Almost none?
* *Plan contingency actions* - Okay. If the most probable events do occur, what could you do to prevent them or reverse them? Specifically? Write down your contingency plan.

How Lloyd H. Made His Venture's Future More Secure

Lloyd H. of Toledo, Ohio, operates a successful sales organization of five salesmen who represent cookware manufacturers in the midwest. Lloyd's list of possibilities looked like this:

One or two salesmen may quit and start their own sales organization.

One of our major suppliers may go out of business and we will be without merchandise.

The economy may take a downturn and stop customers from buying as much from us.

Ill health may force me to sell my business and I'll lose my income.

Each of these four possibilities had to be faced, but Lloyd knew that some of them were less likely to happen than others. Here's how Lloyd planned contingency actions:

Offer salesmen an extra incentive for increased sales to keep the better salesmen.

Look for alternative suppliers in case one of the major suppliers closes up.

Build a cash reserve in case of a change in the economy and find inflation-proof products to sell as a sideline.

Get a physical checkup and take out wage-earner insurance.

Lloyd had the right idea—don't wait for tomorrow, plan for it today. Lloyd's success as a Full-Time Fortune Builder is due, in part, to his ability to plan and act on the future.

BUILDING YOUR WEALTH AS AN ENTREPRENEUR

A Weekend Wealth Builder is actually a part-time *entrepreneur.* An entrepreneur (ON-truh-pruh-NEUR) is someone who starts and operates businesses for a profit; no other reason. He derives his satisfaction from seeing a well-run business. If the business isn't profitable, he quickly sells it and moves on to another.

One of the most successful entrepreneurs I know is Steve W. of Seattle, Washington who operates seven successful businesses from the den of his $160,000 home overlooking beautiful Puget Sound. Steve started small—just as your are—with just one Weekend Wealth Venture, a wooden sign shop in his garage, and built it into a Full-Time Fortune Builder. Then Steve used the profits from his business to start two more businesses—a wooden toy manufacturing company and a marketing service for small business operators.

Steve's salary as a successful entrepreneur is more than $75,000 a year. His secrets? I'll let him pass them along to you:

1. Make your primary goal in business: profit.
2. Don't let emotion overrule your natural common sense. Buy or sell because it makes sense, not just because it would be fun.
3. Always grow. Keep searching for the better way. Learn from your experiences and act on the lessons you've learned from them.

Those are Steve's three steps to becoming a full-time entrepreneur.

DIVERSIFYING YOUR PROFITS
WITH NEW WEALTH VENTURES

One of the greatest insurance policies a smart Weekend Wealth Builder can write is *Diversification Insurance.* It's simply insuring a profitable future by not putting all your nest eggs into one basket. It's like playing roulette and putting your money on both "red" and "black"—you're bound to win. And a smart wealth venture can give you much better than house odds.

You can write your own Diversification Insurance policy by either starting up a brand new Weekend Wealth Venture or by buying one from someone who doesn't have the skills of an entrepreneur like you.

Here's how smart Weekend Wealth Builders diversify their income for security by starting a new and profitable Weekend Wealth Venture:

* Find a need of a large group of potential buyers
* Decide how best to fill it
* Discover whether you can fill the need profitably
* Take action to earn your profit through fulfilling someone's need

Simple enough. As an example, let's see:

How Dorothy R. Wrote Her Own Profitable Diversification Insurance Policy

Dorothy R.'s babysitting syndicate was already highly successful. Parents throughout her hometown of Altoona, Pennsylvania, called her to secure qualified and responsible babysitters for their children. Dorothy would then call one of her employees and notify her of the job. Each of her sitters had been through a short course that Dorothy taught in child care, handling emergencies and other subjects. Dorothy received 20 percent of the babysitter's earnings for the referral.

One day Dorothy decided that she wanted to build her business from a part-time venture into a full-time enterprise using the knowledge she gained from operating her babysitting syndicate for two years. She began looking for a large group of potential users and at what their needs were. Dorothy quickly discovered that she could fill the needs of many of her current customers with a preschool program.

To set up a profitable preschool program, Dorothy would need a large area in her home that was close to kitchen and bathroom facilities yet isolated from the rest of the home. She chose the basement; it was perfect.

But would it be profitable? Dorothy decided that she could operate her preschool program for about 20 children with just one helper. By charging six dollars a day for each child, her income would be 120 dollars a day or 600 dollars a week. She estimated wages for her helper at three dollars an hour for the six hours—18 dollars a day—and other expenses beyond initial setup at about 10 dollars a day. This left Dorothy with a profit, before her wages, of 92 dollars a day!

Dorothy further expanded her income by offering lunches at $1.50 each—basic cost: 50 cents—and weekend abysitting at a nominal cost.

Dorothy's diversification plan worked. She began a new wealth venture that offered a full-time wage that was steadier than on-call babysitting. She still operates her successful babysitting syndicate, but now she has an employee operate it for her.

Dorothy is a smart Full-Time Fortune Builder.

TURNING SOMEONE'S FAILURE INTO YOUR SUCCESS

Once you've put the successful Weekend Wealth Plan into action and proven to yourself that you can make a healthy profit with this simple system, you'll be ready to analyze and improve other ventures profitably. You'll be able to take over and turn around small businesses that are not as successful. You'll be an entrepreneur.

To take over an enterprise and turn it into diversified profits ask yourself these questions:

* How much profit is this venture now making?
* Where is this profit coming from?
* How can the income be increased?
* How can expenses be lowered without lowering the quality of the product or service?
* How can the product or service be improved to satisfy a wider group of customers?
* How can this business' Venture Concept be defined?
* What is the monetary value of this venture in its current condition?
* What type of offer will the owner accept?
* How desperate is the owner to sell?
* Can you offer the owner a percentage of profits or a long-term contract in payment for the venture?
* Will the takeover of this enterprise bring me closer to my own goals?

How Byron H. Used The Weekend Wealth Plan To Turn A Loss Into An Instant Profit

Byron H. found his success operating a book search service that found rare and out-of-print books for clients at a profitable fee. But soon he wanted to turn his knowledge of Smart Management Strategy and the Weekend Wealth Plan into a Full-Time Fortune Builder.

One of Byron's clients was a research service in a nearby metropolitan area. He had found many volumes for them and helped them build their enterprise. In a long talk with the owners of the research service he discovered that they were making only a small profit with their venture and they were considering selling it—accounts and all. Byron began asking questions.

He soon discovered that their fee for research was lower than that of other similar services, that they were concentrating on only a small portion of the market for their service, and that they often purchased reference material for a study that cost more than the study itself paid them. They were operating their venture inefficiently.

Byron made them an offer. For making him an equal partner he would turn their venture around and show them how to increase both their income and their profits. They agreed and by increasing fees, promoting and expanding their service and making their operation more efficient with the Weekend Wealth Plan, Byron turned his knowledge into a hefty profit. Best of all, Byron now spends no more than two hours a week helping his partners operate their venture yet he collects between $300 and $400 in easy profits each month as their partner.

Byron knows how to use his success to breed more success for himself and for others.

MAKING YOUR WEALTH WORK FOR YOU

Once you've found success with my Weekend Wealth Plan you'll be anxious to enjoy some of the easy profits you've earned by working smarter rather than harder. Here's how the nation's most successful Weekend Wealth Builders put their profits to work while they help other venture builders reach their own goals—they Rent Money.

That's right. You can make your money earn more money for you by renting it to people who can multiply it with the Weekend Wealth Plan. You can turn idle cash into extra profits by using:

* *Short-term loans* - Encourage others to use the Weekend Wealth Plan to build their spare time income, then offer to lend them the cash to get

started—at a profitable interest rate. They will appreciate your offer and you will appreciate the 10, 12, 14 percent or more you'll earn on your money.

* *Long-term loans* - You can also help others expand their Weekend Wealth Venture into a Full-Time Fortune Builder with Rented Money. Your cash will be secure in a growing enterprise and you'll receive an extra check every month without lifting a finger.
* *Partnerships* - Many smart Weekend Wealth Builders turn their profits into more business ventures by going into business with other venture builders. They bring the cash and their partners bring important and profitable Wealth Building Blocks. Some successful Weekend Wealth Builders have interest in a half-dozen or more profitable ventures in many fields. They've written a *Diversification Insurance* policy that insures them of an income in any economic climate.

How Brendon Y. Retired At Age 35

Brendon's first Weekend Wealth Venture was simple enough. It was importing children's toys—mostly from Korea. Slowly his profits—and his bank account—grew until he had over $10,000 in the bank. Rather than spend it on luxuries, Brendon decided to reinvest it into the most successful investment he knew of—the Weekend Wealth Plan. Here's how he did it:

First, Brendon talked among his friends encouraging those he trusted to build their own part-time profit ventures. He offered to lend them starting capital at 14 percent interest or work with them as partners. In each case all he required was that they let him offer ideas on how they could increase their profitability. They readily agreed.

Then Brendon used all profits and interest on loans to start more loans and partnerships. He diversified his ventures until he owned portions of more than 17 separate part- and full-time enterprises spread across three states.

Finally, when Brendon reached age 35, he sold his interests in the businesses to his partners on easy-payment plans with the understanding that they would allow him to continue in an advisory capacity—with a small salary. Brendon's salaries from the many ventures *plus* payments from the partners who bought him out *plus* payments from loans still outstanding gave him an income of more than $2,000 a month. He reinvested 25 percent of his income into new loans and partnerships and lives well on the rest.

Brendon Y. is one of many smart Weekend Wealth Builders who decided to expand and diversify his ventures to build a new and more profitable future with the Weekend Wealth Plan.

YOU CAN TURN WEEKENDS INTO WEALTH

You are a success!

You've put the Weekend Wealth Plan into action and turned your spare time into extra cash using a few simple principles and techniques.

You made the smart decision to start your own Weekend Wealth Venture and you took the first important steps toward putting that plan into action.

You soon discovered your own Wealth Building Blocks and realized how you can turn them into easy cash.

You discovered hundreds of unique Weekend Wealth Ventures and learned how to quickly analyze each of them for the greatest profit.

You uncovered dozens of new sources for start-up and expansion capital

You chose the best of many business ideas and expanded them into potential opportunities.

You tested the top venture opportunities on paper and minimized risks *before* they occurred.

You learned the dynamic secrets of producing and distributing your product or service profitably.

You discovered the secrets of Weekend Wealth Builders—of how to increase your income through smart marketing and promotion.

You unraveled the mystery of motivation and how to use it to make others help you build your venture.

You found a wealth of profitable ideas on how to work by priority and eliminate losses from waste.

You pinpointed the secrets of the nation's richest wealth builders: how to increase profits through simple recordkeeping and how to legally avoid taxes.

Finally, you've uncovered the secrets of increasing your wealth through venture expansion and diversification.

Most important, I sincerely hope that this book has taught you that *you* have the power to earn spare time cash and the satisfaction of personal success.

You are now a smart Weekend Wealth Builder.

ENERGIZING YOUR WEEKEND WEALTH PLAN

Now that you've discovered the real key to financial success and security—yourself—do these things today to insure your profitable future:

1. Accept the Weekend Wealth Plan as a comprehensive plan for turning your time and skills into extra cash anytime you want it.
2. Energize your Weekend Wealth Plan by using your own unique powers and talents to reach a clearly defined and realistic goal that will bring you the happiness and satisfaction you deserve.
3. Renew your Weekend Wealth Plan by rereading this book and using its principles to help you develop your own part-time venture toward success.
4. Share the Weekend Wealth Plan with others and help them overcome their natural reluctance to believe in themselves and make their own future.
5. Believe in the Weekend Wealth Plan—and in yourself.

Index